TRAILBLAZERS

"Ultimately, it really doesn't matter how or where you gain insight; it only matters that you do. So, when you encounter a collection of knowledge as worthwhile as "Mind Capture," you really ought to pay attention. Tony's work can unlock your potential. It can change everything... Just as "Think & Grow Rich" inspired that boy back in Indiana, "Mind Capture" will inspire its share of leaders and potential leaders. In fact, I think it's safe to say that someone reading this book will change the world. And, whether or not that person realizes it, this book will have played a part in that accomplishment."

—**Dave Liniger**, Chairman and Co-Founder, RE/MAX, LLC

"A powerfully effective, clear cut guide to addressing and overcoming the adversity and setbacks which are part of every business professional's journey to success. Whether you're just starting a new business endeavor or you've been in the business world for years, this book will revolutionize the way you look at taking risks and equip you with the knowledge, strategies, characteristics, and habits that will catapult you toward sustained success in not only your business but also throughout every aspect of your life."

—**Ivan Misner**, Ph.D., *New York Times* Bestselling Author and Founder of BNI©

"While there are many roadmaps that can help you become successful, it is truly the trailblazers who veer off the paved roads who have the greatest impact. Tony Rubleski has pulled together an amazing group of people who have refused to stay on the road and have, instead, insisted on riding the rough, unpaved terrain to reach their goals. Buckle up for a bumpy ride through the minds of those who prefer to off-road!"

—**Joel Comm**, *New York Times* Bestselling Author and CEO, Joel Comm Inc.

"If you're looking for just another boring business book, this book is not for you. If you're looking for a book that will transform the way you look at marketing, sales, business, and life, then Tony Rubleski has written the book you've been waiting to read. Jam-packed with powerful advice, insights, and recommendations on how to market smarter, sell more, and capture the minds of the people who matter most, this masterful book gives you the keys to unlock your true success. Don't waste another minute. Buy this book NOW."

David Newman, author of #1 bestseller *Do It! Marketing: 77 Instant-Action Ideas to Boost Sales, Maximize Profits, and Crush Your Competition*

"Tony Rubleski has defined Think and "BE" Rich—having grown up on Napoleon Hills LAP believe me I know—with a blueprint everyone can now follow. Trust those who blazed the wealth trails to keep you CURRENT in the SUPER CHANGE markets we reside within. Buy five and share this wealth "driver" with those you REALLY care for... I am."

— **Berny Dohrmann**, Chairman and Founder of CEO Space International and Author of *Super Achiever Mind Sets*

"Leaders are going to want to read and distribute this book to their teams. Tony, curated a quick, powerful, insightful and authentic read; packed with real world, actionable content to immediately improve the lives of his readers."

— **Tim Basa**, Exec. President, Telegration

"It's been said that success leaves tracks, and while successful entrepreneurs understand that while wealth rewards risk, it doesn't mean that every highly successful entrepreneur blazed a new trail or made a new revolutionary discovery—quite the contrary. Being mentored by and learning from other successful business owners, participating in mastermind groups, and reading books like the one you're holding right now are all powerful ways that you can accelerate your path to success.

The stories in this book of innovation, overcoming challenges, and sheer 'gut it out' persistence are a veritable gold mine of wisdom, encouragement and inspiration for new entrepreneurs and seasoned veterans alike. One of the keys to creating your Dream Business is to learn valuable lessons from those who have 'blazed a trail' before you. This book is now your roadmap to success."

— **Jim Palmer**, The Dream Business Coach, www. DreamBizCoaching.com

"An absolutely amazing book jam packed with an abundance of marketing nuggets that will change your life. Your Life will never be the same after you read this book. Get ready for explosive results!"

— **John DiLemme**, Strategic Business Coach and Small Business Expert

"Tony Rubleski is responsible for many of my great friends and for much of my success. This 4th book is Tony's best so far. It contains countless, unique, never revealed success secrets from the world's greatest achievers from all walks of life. Tony helps very successful people discover new things about their own success, and this book will also help the reader to learn things they have not read anywhere else.

Do yourself a favor and tap into the success secrets from these Trailblazers and discover new thinking, processes, and systems to help you get to where you want to be faster and with fewer roadblocks."

— **Tom "too tall" Cunningham**, Napoleon Hill Foundation Certified Instructor

"Just like Think and Grow Rich, Chicken Soup for the Soul, and How to Win Friends and Influence People adorn the bookcases of nearly every successful businessperson; Mind Capture: Leadership Lessons from Ten

Trailblazers Who Beat the Odds and Influenced Millions is worthy of a spot right next to them.

Tony's collection of personal interviews is like a super-concentrated seed for success that, when applied, will produce unfathomable results for the reader. His humorous style of interviewing not only engages and inspires; he also boils down the seemingly complex into simple action-oriented nuggets. Adding to this, he also shares a rare glimpse into the ups and downs of his own life and career that will certainly surprise and inspire others. This book is a MUST READ!"

— **Dave "The Shef" Sheffield**, Author &
Motivational Speaker, www.TheShef.com

"I am honored to be a big part of Tony Rubleski's 4th Mind Capture book for several reasons: First, I even hate to even call it a book in the Mind Capture series. This is a powerful collection of interviews from today's movers and shakers in a broad spectrum of industries…and you, the reader are getting a front row, sneak peek of their very best secrets. Calling them trailblazers is an understatement.

And second, Tony himself is honest about failure and success, and gives you the no BS sense of just how hard it is to start something big …yet how easy it can be if you surround yourself with the right people. I highly recommend Tony's latest work and look forward to reading my colleagues insights as well."

— **Brad Szollose**, Generational Expert, Web Pioneer,
Award-winning author of *Liquid Leadership*

"Tony Rubleski knows how to ask the best people the right questions every time. The ideas and insights you take from this book are priceless. The wisdom contained here is timeless. Use this book to gain the upper hand in your life and business. Thank you, Tony!"

— **Mike Dolpies** (AKA: Mike D) Author & Consultant,
www.CyberspaceToYourPlace.com

"This is a book of innovative leaders who are not afraid to set trends. The common strand among all of the contributors is the way they flip mediocrity to their favor. Mind Capture: Leadership Lessons is about you Thinking, Doing and Being Different than 100% of everyone else while changing the world as an influencer."

— **Darren Monroe**, Consultant to Passionate People Who Profit

"Read and grow wise, irresistible and influential! You're holding the right book. This book will show you how to enjoy the rewards of your perseverance and nurture you through tough times. Blaze your own trails!"

— **Svetlana Kim**, Author, *White Pearl* and *I: A Memoir of a Political Refugee*

"Although a trailblazer has talent and determination, Tony captures and shares the value of a trailblazer's heart."

— **Greg Heeres**, Founder of Maximize

"Every successful person has suffered setbacks. We sometimes forget that as we pursue our dreams. Tony puts us back on the road to success, then he adds the extra gas! Get this book."

— **Frank J. Kenny**, Founder, Chamber Professionals Community

"I have read hundreds and hundreds of books on what it takes to be successful in both your personal & business life, but Tony's newest book "takes the cake". Tony Rubleski is a master interviewer that digs deep into what all of us need to reach the top. How can you lose when you learn from the best like Seth Godin, John Stossel, and Jay Abraham? You need to add reading this book to your bucket list."

— **Tim Green**, Author and International Speaker

"When you get people who already achieved your goals to share their experiences, you can often shortcut the success process. But how do you track down these people and then convince them to reveal their most valuable advice? Tony solves this problem with his book… Thanks to an insightful interviewing style, he gets a world-class group of business leaders to reveal their roads to achievement. More importantly, however, these high-level achievers also detail the setbacks that threatened to detour their rise to the top. What results are lessons that motivate, entertain and inspire."

— **Tom Trush**, President, Write Way Solution, LLC

"This book gives you get the keys to the vault that contains lightning bolts of inspiration and hope when the going gets tough… In addition to Tony, each of these proven successful entrepreneurs pull back the curtain and destroy the myth of the 'get rich quick' and entitlement garbage that many people today still unfortunately buy into.

Living your dream is a constantly evolving work in process. Tony's book helps you to realize how every difficult situation is another opportunity to improve yourself and learn how to better use your talents to help others. Read it, apply it, and observe how it can fuel your fire to live your dreams and bring clarity to your purpose in this life."

— **Brad Brinkman**, Real Estate Sales Trainer, Speaker, and Author

TRAILBLAZERS

*Leadership Lessons from 12 Pioneers
Who Beat the Odds & Influenced Millions*

TONY RUBLESKI

NEW YORK

LONDON • NASHVILLE • MELBOURNE • VANCOUVER

TRAILBLAZERS

Leadership Lessons from 12 Pioneers
Who Beat the Odds and Influenced Millions

Published in New York, New York, by Morgan James Publishing. Morgan James is a trademark of Morgan James, LLC. www.MorganJamesPublishing.com

The Morgan James Speakers Group can bring authors to your live event. For more information or to book an event visit The Morgan James Speakers Group at www.TheMorganJamesSpeakersGroup.com.

ISBN 978-1-68350-873-1 paperback
ISBN 978-1-68350-874-8 eBook
Library of Congress Control Number: 2017918433

In an effort to support local communities, raise awareness and funds, Morgan James Publishing donates a percentage of all book sales for the life of each book to Habitat for Humanity Peninsula and Greater Williamsburg.

Get involved today! Visit
www.MorganJamesBuilds.com

DEDICATION

To God, the ultimate Trailblazer, and the gift of curiosity on this fascinating journey known as life.

CONTENTS

Foreword

BY DAVE LINIGER

Dave Liniger, Chairman and Co-Founder, RE/MAX, LLC

I was introduced to Napoleon Hill's *Think & Grow Rich* as a 16-year-old farm boy in Marion, Indiana. The book had a profound impact on me, and I've reread it more than 50 times over the years. It's fair to say that the foundation of the worldwide RE/MAX real estate network is based on the principles described in this amazing collection of thoughts and strategies.

The book also helped me through a 2012 health crisis that threatened to either kill me or steal my ability to walk. I thought about the lessons of *Think & Grow Rich* virtually every day of my very difficult recovery. Once more, Napoleon Hill had helped me change my life, just as he's done with countless other readers.

Now Tony Rubleski is doing the same thing for a new generation.

The ideas Tony has collected in *Mind Capture* have the power to transform. The only requirements of readers are an open mind, an eagerness to learn, a positive attitude and the will to act upon the strategies being offered.

Fortunately, from an early age I've soaked up life lessons wherever I could find them. Sometimes they came through books. Sometimes through presentations or conversations. Sometimes through experience. And sometimes through tapes or CDs (I've listened to a lifetime of instructional and motivation programs in my car—drive time can be incredibly productive if you're smart with it).

Ultimately, it really doesn't matter *how* or *where* you gain insight; it only matters that you *do*. So, when you encounter a collection of knowledge as worthwhile as *Mind Capture*, you really ought to pay attention. Tony's work can unlock your potential. It can change everything.

One thing to realize about the interviews in Mind Capture is that when you're reading the words of Seth Godin or John Stossel or Brian Tracy, you're getting not only their thoughts, but also the thoughts of those who contributed to their success along the way. In the same way, when you're reading my story, you're getting bits of Napoleon Hill and thousands of others who influenced me.

That's an incredible thing to consider, and it reinforces the immense value of accessing so many great leaders and thinkers in one place. It's one of the truly dynamic aspects of what Tony has accomplished throughout the *Mind Capture* series.

Just as *Think & Grow Rich* inspired that boy back in Indiana, *Mind Capture* will inspire its share of leaders and potential leaders.

In fact, I think it's safe to say that someone reading this book will change the world. And, whether or not that person realizes it, this book will have played a part in that accomplishment.

trail-blaz-er:
1. One who blazes a trail.
2. An innovative leader in a field; a pioneer.

INTRODUCTION

It seems like everywhere you turn, companies and organizations of all shapes and sizes are continually struggling with two interconnected challenges in relation to their employees:

- How do they inspire and lead their teams to greater success?
- How do they foster and encourage their people to step up and lead?

Leadership is a timeless topic. Bookstore shelves are flooded with books about it. There are countless programs, opinions, and perspectives about what effective leadership looks like. In addition, every day, countless new videos, speeches, articles, and blogs are written about it.

I'm often asked from people around the world how they can best achieve greater profits and inspire their people to step up and lead within their respective organizations. I get these queries on phone calls, at keynotes I speak at, and via workshop and best-practice sessions I facilitate with a wide range of business and nonprofit leaders. I wish I could give them a silver-bullet answer, but none exists. However, in the pages of this book, I will pull insight and wisdom on this timeless topic from some of the top leadership minds. I've dubbed them "Trailblazers."

Here are a few key questions to consider as you begin your journey into the book and lessons from the twelve Trailblazers interviewed:

- How will you continue to lead effectively in a lightning-fast world of digital competition?
- What will you do to upgrade your skills to remain relevant and aware of new challenges and opportunities?
- How will you attract key people to work with you and keep the key players from leaving you for a new or better opportunity?
- What do world-class leaders do when adversity strikes?
- What do world-class leaders do to sustain and build from success versus becoming complacent?

Here are a few things you will discover by reading this book and checking out the full audio interview links at the end of each chapter:

- *Leadership lessons to inspire and motivate*
- *The power of faith along the journey*
- *Effective ways to deal with business setbacks*
- *Why a strong mindset is essential to get ahead*
- *Proven ways to reinvent your business, life, and career*
- *Why failure is part of the success process*

- *How to handle adversity and doubt*
- *Time management tips to get more done*

I'm certain that you'll find the wisdom from the twelve Trailblazers interviewed to be of incredible value to not just yourself, but those you currently lead. Each chapter is broken down to highlight key takeaways and thoughts. This will save you time and serve as a catalyst and reminder that great leadership is a learnable trait. People are not born leaders. This book will help you quickly realize that leadership is a very learnable skill and often born of lots of trial and error. The key benefit you the reader will gain is a bird's-eye view and shortcut from these leaders who poured out their wisdom, good and bad, during our time together.

How This Book Came to Be

The genesis of the book started with a phone call a few years ago. I was on the phone with business coach and fellow author Jim Palmer discussing life, goals, and, in particular, my next book in the *Mind Capture* series. I had an idea of where the next book would go, while he had another.

For many months, I'd been thinking that the next book would be about dealing with setbacks and the steps one must take in the mental battle to overcome them. At the time of our phone call, I was emerging from great change. As my inner circle of close friends, family, and business associates already knew, I'd seen enough chaos, change, and unforeseen disruption the two years prior to make moving forward seem like a pipedream. I'm not proud of all of it, however looking back now, it was painful and necessary to break free to allow for positive growth in many aspects of my personal and business life. It forced me to address serious and long overdue changes on multiple fronts.

As you read this, I'm certain you can relate to dealing with temporary setback and change. When life throws intense challenges and adversity your way, it will often test every ounce of mental, physical, and spiritual muscle you thought you ever had, while at the same time it will pull out great reserves of ingenuity and untapped creativity that were hidden within you. Once you get some time to look back on the challenge, you're often shocked at how far along you've come for the better.

The Good News:
We're Allowed to Reinvent Ourselves Each Day, Forgive Ourselves and Others, and Shut the Door to the Past

Many of you can relate to what I'm saying. Maybe it's the loss of a loved one, a business, a dream, a child, a job you loved, or some other sucker punch like a cancer diagnosis that completely throws you for a loop. It knocks you down many times in mind, spirit, and body and tries to keep you stuck there. However, as the pain recedes, the confidence and momentum can return if we forgive, grow, and change our thinking. When this happens, life and passion can return and we heal forward into a new season of life. One season ends and another one starts anew. We're never quite the same as time, growth, new people, and wisdom have reshaped us into a much different person.

So, back to my phone call with Jim. As we wrapped up our intense conversation, my direction for the original book I had planned to write did a complete 180. I'd almost forgotten that there existed an incredible goldmine of wisdom and success strategies in my laptop and saved audio files that I had compiled over the last seven years from many of the best sales, marketing, leadership, and newsmakers on the planet.

This goldmine of wisdom contained over eighty-plus taped phone interviews that I'd compiled for my paid monthly newsletter subscribers over the last seven years. Since I'm always under multiple deadlines, I'd frankly taken for granted the wisdom, tips, and inspiration contained in the interviews with my trailblazing and highly enlightened guests.

Why Positive Influences Are So Important, Especially Today

Let's face it: We ALL need more positive influences and people in our daily lives. I've had many people tell me, "Tony, those interviews you do are incredible!" While it would be easy to sit on my press clippings and fanfare, I'm at a point in life where that's no longer my primary driver for serving others. My core mission or "why" is big, bold, direct, and massive: to expose millions of people per year to positive, life-changing information.

The media landscape is built on fear and controversy. Complaining is epidemic and toxic. Blame is the new game. Add in a growing push for entitlement at all levels of government and within the media, and the "something for nothing" syndrome is putting more people within society on edge. It's not a conspiracy or a paranoid dream. It's happening, and people are waking up!

I see it around the world, at my events, and on conference calls as the game of fear is being exposed. People know that deep down something has gone astray. They've ignored their intuition too long, buried their dream, and allowed the fear peddlers to sell them a vision of life that no longer makes any sense. After years of societal programming and norms that no longer work in a digital-based open world, the addiction to negativity and the traditional job/career/retire-after-thirty-years career model has been exposed and dismantled especially by the twenty to thirty-year-old crowd. Frankly, most people are sick of the old model and looking for ways to improve their life, those they love, and others they'd like to serve with greater reach and impact.

Why This Book at This Moment in Time?

Let's go back in time for a brief moment to set the stage for the book you now hold in your hand or display on your computer or ebook reader screen. The last several years I've been blessed to pick the minds of many of the top leaders, thinkers, and influencers on the planet. The time I share during the interview with my guests and the research involved in the process is valuable for everyone involved.

I still get a charge out of interacting and engaging with my special guests and never take their time and wisdom for granted. Each of them has a unique story and a journey that teaches us lessons from both sides of the wheel of life when it seems everything is clicking, or when it seems all hope of achieving our goal seems too far away or even impossible.

Each person interviewed in the book comes from diverse, eclectic, and oftentimes mundane backgrounds. The commonality that they ALL share, however, is massive amounts of persistence! What would knock ninety-nine out of 100 people out of the game doesn't stop them from pressing on. With relentless intensity, the pull to achieve is simply too strong, and eventually, after years of toil, sweat, heartache, and an emotional roller coaster, many of them "arrive," to the surprise of the casual observer. Even with the chorus of dream-stealers, doubters, and sadly, the criticism of those nearest, including families and friends, they persisted onward through thick and thin.

The road to their seemingly overnight success is oftentimes littered with years of failed enterprises, tears, and pain from many outdated relationships that simply couldn't handle the stress brought on by lack of security, a steady paycheck, and maxed-out credit cards. This is the side of being an entrepreneur that few talk about. In addition, the "crazy idea" they chased was even more tempting to leave when a steady job with benefits was often simply a phone call or email away because eager employers were looking for someone with their talent and drive to work for their organization.

For example, when the accolades come and success finally arrives in the eighth year of being in business, it's amazing how quickly people want to skip over or ignore the first seven years of the story. Those were the lean years, when few, if anyone, that knew what they were really up to believed in them. The amazing thing is that as they persisted and made adjustments along the journey, they were also being forged from raw iron (their vision) into steel (the successful outcome).

The last several years I've been extremely fortunate and blessed to pick the brains of some of the brightest minds on the planet ranging from the fields of sales, marketing, psychology, to sports, music, and spirituality. It hasn't come easy to "capture" these incredible minds on the phone. I put in the time, the discipline, the miles, the thousands of pages read, to do my homework and establish a track record with busy PR handlers and agents. The mission is to make them look good while at the same time ensuring that my guest feels relieved that they didn't waste their time.

Within the first five minutes, each guest knows that our interview will be different than most others they often do. I know this to be true as I also get interviewed by others as an author myself. By the end of our time together, I want to have pulled out not only multiple nuggets of wisdom for my audience but also something so unique that it leaves them thinking, *Damn, I did not expect that. That was unique, engaging, and memorable.*

Here's the secret that shocks most people that ask me about my guests: They are regular people, just like you and me, who have achieved massive success in their respective fields. They all had to start somewhere and oftentimes it was during times of great chaos and setback taking place within their own lives that they made the **big decision** to cut the cord and go full throttle after their big goal or dream. Nothing was given to them. They had to hustle, deal with lots of rejection, and bust through the paradigms of what a long line of others said couldn't be done. They also had to face down and conquer the twin enemies known as fear and self-doubt oftentimes for years in relative obscurity and during multiple setbacks. During this process, each of them grew, blazed a trail, and changed millions of lives along the way for the better.

While each Trailblazer is unique and talented in their own way, I went back through this book several times and realized that they all share a few commonalities worth noting. The checklist below with seven key characteristics they possess isn't a magical shortcut to success, but a blueprint of consistent behaviors and habits one will likely need in the pursuit of their own major goal or dream. The list also serves as a powerful reminder that a positive mindset is of monumental importance.

Seven Key Characteristics ALL These Trailblazers Have in Common:

#1: **Intense curiosity**

#2: **Persistence**

#3: **Vision**

#4: **Lifelong learners**

#5: **Problem solvers**

#6: **Focus on their strengths**

#7: **Thick skin**

What Else You Will Discover in This Book and Full Audio Interviews

- *The twin allies known as persistence and belief*
- *The power of vision, goal setting, and affirmations*
- *How to think like a trailblazer*
- *How to grow a business in any economy*
- *Proven ways to turn your ideas into reality*
- *The power of the mastermind and key strategic business alliances*
- *How to live life on your own terms*
- *Why you must guard your mind from negative people, news, and gossip*
- *Additional books, resources, and groups you should know about*

- *Effective ways to collaborate and work with others*
- *Proven ways to get people to pay attention to your ideas*
- *How to understand and effectively use social media within your business*

In an age of mobile phones, social media, and short-attention spans, you'll also discover in this book and via the "Captured Wisdom" audio interview links contained at the end of each chapter, multiple ways to access and retain the wisdom from each Trailblazer interview.

Once again, I was fortunate to extract, capture, and share this valuable wisdom with my original audience of newsletter subscribers and fans of *Mind Capture* the last few years. Now with this book, these interviews are being shared on a much larger global scale.

How to Get the Most Out of This Book and the Audio Interviews

Each chapter is broken down for maximum enjoyment, retention, and learning into five areas:

1. A quick look at each Trailblazer
2. A few key highlights from our interview
3. A list of five key "Mind Nuggets" or quotes to ponder and reflect upon
4. A quick review of additional areas discussed in the full audio interview and a link to access and listen to the audio interview in its full entirety
5. More information at the end of the chapter on each Trailblazer

Thank you again for your time and investment in this life-changing knowledge. It is up to you to choose wisely, take notes, study, and apply these lessons within your own life.

Here's a quick thought to consider and inspire you from one of the featured Trailblazer's in chapter two, Dave Liniger, cofounder of the real estate juggernaut RE/MAX:

"Mind Capture *will inspire its share of leaders and potential leaders. In fact, I think it's safe to say that someone reading this book will change the world. And, whether or not that person realizes it, this book will have played a part in that accomplishment."*

Now, buckle up for the exciting journey to discover valuable wisdom from these unique Trailblazers who beat the odds and influenced millions!

Chapter 1
SETH GODIN

"What the Internet is doing is many things, but one of them is completely undermining the system."
—Seth Godin

Big Picture Trailblazer

They say that lightning rarely strikes twice. Well, I must say that getting Seth Godin to do a second interview certainly felt like it. Yes, Seth Godin is in a league of his own. When you read his body of work, it shows not only range but genius on multiple fronts ranging from marketing and history to economics and sociology. If I had to make a list of ten people who've influenced my career the most, he'd easily be on it.

With his book *The Icarus Deception*, he deconstructs the old way of work and the Industrial Age and how each of us can thrive in the new connection-based economy. Yes, a tall task. A complex topic. Strong opinions. Lots of dots to connect and synthesize. Perfect for someone like Seth Godin.

The three main things I enjoy most about Seth's writing and message include:

1. Seth's style is engaging, makes you think, and always questions the status quo.
2. He shares why we're all artists now and how the global economy will reward or punish those who understand this major shift in socio economic thinking.
3. The wisdom and raw honesty of his own stories, career, fears, and wins is not only revealing but inspiring.

Key Highlights from Our Interview

Tony: You mention in your new book, *The Icarus Deception*, that we're all artists. You and I understand that . . . (but) what do you mean by artist for someone who may have pigeonholed their old definition of the industrial title?

Seth: Don't confuse art and painting, please. A painting might be a work of art, but it probably isn't. It's probably a copy or inspired directly by something else. Art is the work of a human being who is doing something that might not work—something personal and something generous.

You can go to the Avis counter after a long flight to rent a car, and you can interact with someone who is playing it by the book. That person is basically a human cog in an industrial machine. Or, you can go to that counter and find a human being who is looking you in the eye, who is engaging with you, who is talking to you as if you matter. That person in that moment is doing a form of art because it's touching us. It's bringing us closer together. She is saying something that might not work but probably will. When we put ourselves in that position of mattering, putting our name on it, saying to someone, "I made this," we're being artists.

Tony: Amazing . . . Seth, let's talk about the title of the book. It's the old classic mythology, but I like how you explained where you came up with *The Icarus Deception*.

Seth: I was really surprised when I read a 150-year-old copy of the *Myth of Icarus* because it was not what you and I were taught in school or at bedtime. In 1500, and 1600, and 1750, if you heard the story of Icarus, what you would hear is the following: Icarus and his father, Daedalus, were isolated on an island by one of the gods, and his father, who was an inventor, took feathers from birds, wove them into wings, and made a set for him and his son.

And he affixed—they always used the word "affixed"—he affixed the wings to the son's back and said, "We're going to fly away. But there are two rules. Rule number one, don't fly too high because the sun will melt your wax and you will die. And rule number two, Icarus, no matter what, do not fly too low, because if you fly too low the waves and the mists will weigh down your wings and you will surely perish."

What was interesting was that starting around 1800, we started leaving out the second part and the reason is the culture wants people to fly too low. The culture wants the story to be a story about obedience, not a story about possibility.

What I wanted to get across in this book, which is a hard thing to sell people on, is that we are flying too low. It feels like we're doing the best we can in the face of the economy blah, blah, blah. But basically, we're scared and we're flying too low.

Tony: You talk about some things that are important now. I'm going to list them, and I'd like to hear which are your favorites. You talk about trust, permission, remarkability, leadership, stories that spread, and humanity connection. Why are they valuable today?

Seth: If we're leaving the industrial economy and entering the connection economy, where value is created through connection and our ability to do things with one another, whom are we going to connect with? We are not going to connect with a selfish person because they just take. We're going to connect with a generous person because it helps both of us. We're not going to connect with a person we don't trust. We're going to connect to a person that we trust.

But, as we connect to these people, they need leaders. So, when we think about what skills are important to us, they are not the skills of scarcity. "I have a machine that's faster than your machine to make widgets." They are the skills and, actually, it should come with abundance, the abundance of choice, the abundance of connection, the abundance of trust. The more you trust people, the more it is created.

Abundance is a bonus there. It is not a minute you are paying for, and what we have to do is figure out how to change our mindset, because if you are insisting on scarcity and keeping things a secret and being selfish and taking what you can off the table, no one will choose to connect with you. If no one connects with you, you're not going to win.

Tony: So, I'm drawing a parallel there, and what I love about your writing is you are not afraid to push people to think. In my estimate, you started out many years ago as a marketing guru and you shifted much more into the social-economic scene. This whole game is crumbling whether you choose to believe it or not. Again, that's why every time I interview I'm glad the book is moving. It's spreading. And you also give some practical tips for those that are new to the artist way, so I thank you for that and move into this tough one: Why are critics so dangerous to fellow artists like you and me?

Seth: What critics are is the physical embodiment of the lizard brain, right? The critic is busy using exactly the same voice that the voice in your head is using when it told you not to ship the thing in the first place. So, it reinforces and it amplifies, and no one ever built a statue to a critic for a reason, which is that when it's all said and done, we remember Van Gogh. We don't remember the critics who said he had no talent.

Tony: True.

Seth: When all is said and done, we remember Winston Churchill, not the critics who said he didn't know what he was doing. Yet, we give the critics space in our media, and now thanks to public social media, everyone can be a critic. Everyone can criticize. It's easy to see anything that's said and come up with a snarky 140-character rejoinder to it. Some people who are critics get applause for being critics, and so they do it more.

We have created this culture where it's okay to be a critic. I would be humiliated and embarrassed to be called a critic. But there are plenty of people who seem to think that that's their role. The only thing the artist can do is walk away from it, not engage with it, and not try to teach these people a lesson, because there are an endless number of them. You will never be able to drown them out. But as soon as we start ignoring them and get back to our first principles of making work that might not work and being able to say to the critic, "Sorry, it wasn't for you," it helps us open the door to do the work we're capable of.

Tony: Keep shipping that great art, my friend. Time for a final question? Can we do one more?

Seth: Yes sir.

Tony: All right. As you look at your career, you've done a lot. You were on *Entrepreneur* magazine's cover a couple of months ago for *Icarus Deception*. If you fast-forward and someone said, "What do you want your art to be remembered for," what would you say to them?

Seth: I would like to be measured by how much the people who have learned from me have taught other people.

Tony: Interesting. I like it. It's brief. I would not expect anything less from you to keep it provocative. Ladies and gentlemen, we've had the honor to interview again Seth Godin, author of multiple international bestsellers. His latest is *The Icarus Deception*. Pick it up, and be prepared to have your mind expanded. Seth, anything else for us?

Seth: Just thank you, Tony. Keep leading the way. It matters a lot.

Five Key "Mind Nuggets" from Seth to Ponder and Reflect Upon

1. *"What the Internet is doing is many things, but one of them is completely undermining the system."*

2. *"What I have found is that there's a lot of desire to ignore the way the world is changing."*

3. *"What I wanted to get across in this book, which is a hard thing to sell people on, is we are flying too low. It feels like we're doing the best we can in the face of the economy . . . But, basically, we're scared and we're flying too low."*

4. *"Grit is the artist saying, 'Nope, we're not going to do it that way!' Grit is someone sticking it out when it doesn't seem to be working. Grit is the wherewithal to have it match the vision you have in your head. If you're just going to go along to get along, you're not going to get any . . . but you don't have any grit."*

5. *"If we're leaving the industrial economy and entering the connection economy, where value is created through connection and our ability to do things with one another, whom are we going to connect with? We are not going to connect with a selfish person because they just take. We're going to connect with a generous person because it helps both of us."*

What Else Seth Revealed During Our Interview

Here are a few more of the areas we discussed during our *Captured Wisdom* audio interview, which can be accessed at www.mindcapturebook.com/interviews:

- *Why we're all artists now especially in the Internet-based economy*
- *How to handle the resistance to push ahead and get more done*
- *The story and lesson behind the book's title that most people overlook*
- *What industrial propaganda is and how it impacts each one of us*
- *The shift to the connection economy and why it's important to embrace*
- *The power of grit to help you persist onward in the face of doubt and critics*
- *Advice for today's youth on how to shift from industrialist to artist*
- *Why trust, permission, remarkability, leadership, stories that spread, and humanity connection are valuable today*

About Big Picture Trailblazer, Seth Godin

SETH GODIN is the author of 18 books that have been bestsellers around the world and have been translated into more than 35 languages. He writes about the post-industrial revolution, the way ideas spread, marketing, quitting, leadership and most of all, changing everything. You might be familiar with his book Linchpin, Tribes, The Dip, and Purple Cow.

He was recently inducted into the Direct Marketing Hall of Fame, one of three chosen for this honor in 2013.

His newest book, What To Do When It's Your Turn, is already a bestseller.

For more information visit:
sethgodin.com

CHAPTER 2
DAVE LINIGER

"Bravado is pretty easy when you have friends around and the sun is shining. In the middle of the night, looking at the ceiling in a hospital, you're thinking, 'Oh my God. What happens if I'm paralyzed for life? What happens if I can never feed myself again? What if I can't work?' That's what really gets tough."

—**Dave Liniger**

Persistence Trailblazer

It's not every day that you get a chance to interview a business legend who single handedly disrupted an entire industry. This thought-provoking one-on-one interview with RE/MAX founder Dave Liniger is not only inspiring, but loaded with a ton of wisdom and insight.

The first time I spoke with Dave on the phone in August 2012, I was amazed at not only how personable he was, but frankly that he was still alive. A routine back surgery many months earlier had nearly cost him his life, and he awoke four months after the surgery from a long coma. Not only did it nearly take his life, but it also paralyzed his once active body.

In this second interview conducted six months later, we discussed not only his then-new book titled *My Next Step: An Extraordinary Journey of Healing and Hope,* but also the continued growth and recovery he's seen not only in his personal life but within RE/MAX as well. His zest for life and "can-do" attitude is evident throughout the interview as he revealed many success gems that translate over to any business or endeavor.

The three main things I enjoyed most about my interview with Dave include:

1. Dave didn't sugarcoat that to be successful, hard work and persistence are musts.
2. He spoke with candor and honesty and has a sense that the company's impact to positively help others is a major priority.
3. He's never lost a sense of his roots and humility from his early days of working on the farm in Indiana to building one of the largest real estate franchise companies in the world.

Key Highlights from Our Interview

Tony: Let's go back a little bit and talk about the early years of RE/MAX to set the stage, and then we'll fast-forward into the book. Talk about how you started the company and some of the challenges, Dave, that you had in the early years.

Dave: We founded the company in 1973. It was a fairly new and exciting concept in the real estate industry. Traditionally, Realtors split their commissions with the broker of the company or with the office in a 50/50 split. The company used their part of the commission to pay the overhead— secretary, advertising, rent—and make a profit. The agent used their half to pay their own personal overhead like automobile, health insurance, and that type of thing. Then they kept the balance for their income.

What we did was said, let's organize the company like a group of doctors, lawyers, architects who share the expenses of running the company and then keep the vast majority of the fees for themselves. Not an unusual cooperative system—just not used successfully in the real estate business.

Tony: Now, Dave, what did you find? I'm sure the industry did not roll out the red carpet, but how did you deal with the adversity? I've got to think you took some heat for many years. How did you push through in the early days when people said it couldn't be done?

Dave: We had two or three major problems. First, the status quo— the powerful business leaders in the real estate business did not want to see us succeed. If we did, it meant they would lose their top agents to us or be forced to pay them a higher commission split.

The second problem we had, obviously, was my own lack of managerial talent or experience, which certainly was a difficult thing to get over. Then, finally, the skepticism of the agents we were trying to recruit. They all said, "Boy, this sounds good on paper. If it works, I'll join you someday, but I'm not going to leave the company I'm at now for a maybe."

Tony: Let's fast-forward. I'm delighted to really dig into your new book titled *My Next Step*. Early 2012, it's late January, and something forever changed your life that happened that really will guide our conversation today in your new book. What happened to you in that time frame of late January 2012?

Dave: I was on a speaking tour throughout the United States. I was in Galveston, Texas, preparing to give a speech the next morning. I went to bed, and my back had been giving me fits. I needed back surgery and had put it off for two years. My surgeon was a great surgeon. He said, "Let's try some steroid shots, and let's see if we can put off cutting as long as we can." I just felt like my back was finally going out.

I woke up at two in the morning paralyzed from the waist down. I wasn't terribly frightened. I just figured, well, *I've got a slipped disc or some kind of pressure there. I guess I'm going to have back surgery.* I sent a text to my friends and said, "When you guys get up, would you come to my room and unlock me and get me into a hospital?" I asked my CEO, Margaret Kelly, and I said, "By the way, I think you're giving my speech today."

So, they rushed me to a hospital. They got a corporate plane in and picked me up and took me to Sky Ridge Hospital in Denver near where I live. I was admitted. They gave me lots of shots for the pain—several shots of morphine—and I was just about as happy as could be. I went to sleep thinking, *Okay, tomorrow I'll get back surgery, and a week from now I'll be home and starting therapy.* The only problem was I didn't wake up for four months.

Tony: That's amazing. I want to read an excerpt here, which will take me to the next question. It says, "Bravado works fine with the sunlight shining through the windows in daytime, but it quickly disappears at one in the morning when no one else is around and unimaginable terror starts to seep into your mind."

Dave, it takes me to this question: Why is it so essential to have a good support system during the healing process? Explain that.

Dave: What really happens is that you need all of the support you can. This goes back to *Think and Grow Rich* by Napoleon Hill, talking about having a mastermind group or a support group to encourage you. The comment I made was that, with a lot of bravado, when I did wake up I looked at all of the doctors and nurses and friends, and I said, "Get this straight: I might be paralyzed today, but I will walk out of this hospital."

Bravado is pretty easy when you have friends around and the sun is shining. In the middle of the night, looking at the ceiling in a hospital, you're thinking, *Oh my God. What happens if I'm paralyzed for life? What happens if I can never feed myself again? What if I can't work?* That's what really gets tough.

The medical staff are very careful not to overpromise for a couple reasons. One, they don't want a false expectation and seeing you disappointed, but two, they don't want to get sued. If they say, "Yeah, man, we're sure you're going to walk again," and you don't, then somebody might sue them saying, "Well, you said I was going to. I should be able to. You've done something wrong."

The medical staff says, "Dave, we hope for the best but we train you for the worst, and we'll see how you progress." My friends, on the other hand, with a lot of bravado, would say, "Dave, of course you're walking out of this place. You've achieved every goal you wanted. You're going to make it, buddy." Maybe something in between was proper, but I needed both ways.

Tony: You talk about Jack Canfield, another one of the modern day . . . "agents of positive change." I interviewed him many years ago, and his book *Success Principles* struck a chord like it did for you with me. He talks about event plus response equals outcome. How did this influence your recovery? You provided a real good example of how it touched you and helped you in the recovery room.

Dave: I have immersed myself in personal development for fifty years, and I've read just about everything you can read. Canfield's book was absolutely one of my most favorite. He gave the example of an event happens and it's up to your response to determine what your outcome is. At one point, I was so much in despair, semiconscious. I rolled over and I thought, *I just want to die.*

Who knows? Later that night, I gave myself a little pep talk. I got out of my pity party and I said, *for crying out loud. You've been giving motivational speeches for fifty years about never quitting, being persistent, making step-by-step goals and making it. I'm not giving up. E+R=O. The event is I've got a critical spinal injury that has left me paralyzed. My response is, well, I may be a paraplegic, but when I leave this hospital, I'll be the best paraplegic they've ever had.*

And the outcome was positive attitude. I made my step-by-step goals, and it was an inch at a time. I worked harder in therapy than anybody in the hospital. My friends, my family, my therapists encouraged me. The outcome is I am now walking. I still use a cane most of the time.

My goal had been if I could just get out of my wheelchair and walk ten feet. That was my mantra: "Walk ten feet." If you're in an electric power chair and you're paralyzed, the mobility of ten feet is unbelievable. You can get out of a bed by yourself and get into your wheelchair. You can get out of your wheelchair and stand in a shower. You don't have to have a wheelchair van. You can move your wheelchair up to the door, stand up, get in the car, and drive someplace. That was my dream.

Then, as I said slyly at my convention here a couple months ago, "And if I could walk ten feet, boy, I bet I could figure out how to walk 100. And if I can walk 100, I can walk 1,000." As it is now, I'm over 800 feet nonstop. Memorial Day is my test. I am going to try for my 1,000 feet for the first time.

Tony: Dave, you have never quit in your life. Above and beyond the RE/MAX story, your whole life has been about perseverance. But it crossed your mind—and what I like about the book particularly—is (that) you reveal the highs and lows of life.

Let me read this. This is just so powerful. You say, "There were so many people fighting to keep me alive, giving of themselves in unimaginable ways, and all I was thinking about now was giving up."

As you put it in your mind, you were thinking, *that makes you the worst kind of hypocrite. If you give up now, you will wash away forty years of delivering speeches to tens of thousands of people, encouraging them to never give up, to deal with whatever obstacles have been put in their way, to find the courage to face those obstacles head on.*

And I love this. You say, "Screw it. I won't quit. Not now, not ever!"

Wow. Enlighten us on that philosophy when the light switched where you said, "I've had enough. It's time to change."

Dave: Well, you know, the bravado came back. I got my swagger back and stopped feeling sorry for myself. I laid there and I thought about how hypocritical I was and that (after) all the wars I had fought and won getting to where I had in life, and now I would just give up because I was too old and just too tired to continue on.

I just said, "No. My lifetime philosophy has been I'm not the sharpest knife in the drawer, I'm not the smartest person around, but I can outwork anybody." I just thought, "Okay, I've been dealt this deck of cards. I'm going to play them. I will outwork everybody in this hospital and do the absolute best I can to recover the most I can."

Tony: Dave, what I also love is there's a lot of wisdom about success in life and in business. It takes me into a quote that your son mentions. You call him Junior. I want to read it. It's very quick. You always said to your kids: "Small failures, amazing achievements." Explain a little bit more.

Dave: I found in my life that I've learned more from my failures than I have from my successes. A lot of times the successes, you daydream and think you're the reason you're successful, and sometimes there was some luck involved.

On the failures, sure, sometimes there's some bad luck involved, but for the most part, if you sit down and don't point fingers at everybody else, you can start figuring out what you did wrong, and then you just say, "I'm not going to do that again."

It's just like if you ever put your hand onto something that's really hot, like a stove or a stick that's glowing or something, you never do that again. That is going to be indelibly etched into your brain of,

"That is not something I want to do." Learn from the mistakes. Don't fret over them. Don't dwell on them forever. Just say, "Man, I'm not doing that again."

Tony: Dave, what I also love is there's a lot of wisdom about success in life and in business. It takes me into a quote that your son mentions. You call him Junior. I want to read it. It's very quick. You always said to your kids: "Small failures, amazing achievements." Explain a little bit more.

Dave: I found in my life that I've learned more from my failures than I have from my successes. A lot of times the successes, you daydream and think you're the reason you're successful, and sometimes there was some luck involved.

On the failures, sure, sometimes there's some bad luck involved, but for the most part, if you sit down and don't point fingers at everybody else, you can start figuring out what you did wrong, and then you just say, "I'm not going to do that again."

It's just like if you ever put your hand onto something that's really hot like a stove or a stick that's glowing or something, you never do that again. That is going to be indelibly etched into your brain of, "That is not something I want to do." Learn from the mistakes. Don't fret over them. Don't dwell on them forever. Just say, "Man, I'm not doing that again."

It's for the single mom that's raising a couple of kids and working two jobs and she finds the ability to put twenty dollars in the plate at church to be able to help somebody else. That's true generosity. A lot of times, you don't have money when you're younger, but you have time.

Just as somebody with excess money can say, "Here's X many million dollars for this big hospital project," a youngster that's going to college that doesn't have extra money could say, "You know what? I could volunteer one evening a week at the nursing home or at the children's home, and I can give up two to four hours of my time." That donation of time and caring is just as important as the wealthy persons who says, "I have all this money I don't need."

Tony: Wow. Dave Liniger, thank you so much for your time, talent, and treasures. This book is amazing. I'm grateful that we had a chance to get you back on the phone again. I look forward to seeing you and the team again. Thank you to Bruce as well for setting the interview up. Continue the great work you're doing, my friend, okay?

Dave: It will be a pleasure, partner. You take care.

Five Key "Mind Nuggets" from Dave to Ponder and Reflect Upon

1. *"If you have enough perseverance, if there's enough continuity to what you do every day, eventually you do make a success of it."*

2. *A lot of people thought I was a kook, but I had heard that people can often hear you and repeat word for word what you say when they wake up out of a coma at some point. I played motivational tapes. I played a lot of good music."*

3. *"Later that night, I gave myself a little pep talk. I got out of my pity party and I said,* for crying out loud. You've been giving motivational speeches for fifty years about never quitting, being persistent, make step-by-step goals and make it. I'm not giving up. E+R=O. The event is I've got a critical spinal injury that has left me paralyzed. My response is, well, I may be a paraplegic, but when I leave this hospital, I'll be the best paraplegic they've ever had."

4. *"My lifetime philosophy has been I'm not the sharpest knife in the drawer, I'm not the smartest person around, but I can outwork anybody." I just thought,* Okay, I've been dealt this deck of cards. I'm going to play them.

5. *"If you've got the ability to stand up, if you've got your eyesight, if you've got your hearing, you have incredible wealth that literally millions of people who have lost those things don't have. Health is*

the first step to wealth, and the person who has their health—even though they be penniless or broke with money—if you've got your health, you've got a future."

What Else Dave Revealed During Our Interview

Here are a few more of the areas we discussed during our *Captured Wisdom* audio interview, which can be accessed at www.mindcapturebook.com/ interviews:

- *Why personal development is so important in the success process*
- *The power of vision and courage when challenged by competition*
- *The power of the mastermind and why he's such a fan of the book Think and Grow Rich*
- *How the success equation E + R = O, which he learned from Jack Canfield, helped turn his recovery around*
- *Why a strong work ethic is often more important than book smarts*
- *Why the balance between work and play is challenging but necessary for long-term success*
- *The insight gained from learning from our failures if viewed with the right perspective*

About Persistence Trailblazer, Dave Liniger

Dave first became interested in real estate after successfully buying and selling properties to supplement his income while in the Air Force, stationed in Phoenix, Arizona. After working for both a 100% commission company and a traditional brokerage, he co-founded RE/MAX in 1973. Dave's career has put him all over the place. He has been featured in Entrepreneur, Forbes, Fortune, Inc., Success Magazine and many other leading publications and outlets across the globe.

Since 1992, RE/MAX has been the official real estate sponsor of Children's Miracle Network Hospitals. They have also been a sponsor of

the Susan G. Komen for the Cure since 2002. He is currently the CEO,
Chairman, and Co-Founder of RE/MAX.

For more information visit:

remax.com

CHAPTER 3

WM. PAUL YOUNG

"One of the things that I love about story, fiction, poetry, music, creation—one of the things I love is that all of these creative things have a way of slipping into the precious places of the heart without asking for permission, and they give this marvelous entrée, an ability to form your thinking in picture kinds of language."
—Wm. Paul Young

Spirit Trailblazer

If I had to pick my favorite interview I've conducted the past several years, I would say that without a doubt it was my interview with mega-bestselling author Wm. Paul Young, who penned the classic book *The Shack*, which has sold over fifteen million copies.

I remember in the early fall of 2012 assembling a list of twelve great reads for 2012 and pulling the book off my shelf. After I selected it, I had a strange prompting to look up the author to take a complete long-shot to see if I might be able to get a phone interview. As I practice and teach ALL my clients, "You never know until you ask!"

Well, watch what you wish for. I was floored the day before Thanksgiving when I received a long-lost email response from several weeks earlier directly from Paul that read:

Thanks so much for the interview request, something that I am very open to doing with you. Fun!

Please note the better email . . . yours almost got lost in the 3,500 I am behind. :-)

Blessings rich in tenderest grace,

paul

Based on Paul's email, I'd wager to say that securing an interview was nothing short of a miracle based on how many messages and interview requests he receives on a daily basis from around the globe.

I had read the book *The Shack* a few years ago when my then-minister suggested we read it during the holidays. I was amazed by the book's emotion and storyline, but more importantly its powerful message. When you read this book, you'll most likely end up looking at the world and spiritual matters in a more positive and very different way.

The three main things I enjoyed most about my interview with Paul include:

1. Paul shared a few amazing stories from readers and how the book helped them put their life in a positive direction. I call them miracles, but you can be the judge of that if you listen in to our interview.

2. He shared about the struggles he and his family went through before and during the writing of the book. He didn't let the

setbacks of life stop him from living and, thankfully, from writing this book, which has huge global reach and impact.

3. Paul displayed an incredible sense of humility and humor. He was not only down to earth, but he seemed just as shocked as many others in the publishing industry that the book took off like it did. He is a kind soul that deeply cares.

Key Highlights from Our Interview

Tony: So, I want to start from the beginning. Take us back in time and give our global audience some perspective of how you conceived the book *The Shack* and how the book really got traction and got picked up.

Paul: Well, you know, I never tried to publish anything. It never even crossed my mind to do it. You know, I'm figuring, well my friends and my family, they love what I write, but it's because they love me. So, it was never a part of the thought process at all.

Kim, my wife, had been asking me for about four years. Basically, this was the mandate: "Someday, would you please, as a gift for your children— (and we have six, our youngest is eighteen and our oldest is thirty-one)—as a gift to our children, would you someday please put in one place how you think because you think outside the box." Now, she didn't anticipate that that would be a book.

Later actually when the book was eventually for real published, which was in 2007, she said, "You know, when I asked you to do that, I was thinking, you know, four to six pages." She didn't ask me to do that. So, in 2005, which was the year I turned fifty, I thought, *you know what, I am finally, I think, healthy enough as a human being to actually take a shot at this, to put in one place how I think as a gift for my kids, because what would I want to say to them if they're not here.*

One of the things that I love about story, fiction, poetry, music, creation—one of the things I love is that all of these creative things have a way of slipping into the precious places of the heart without asking for permission, and they give this marvelous entrée, an ability to form your thinking in picture kinds of language. Pictures are always, you know, worth a thousand words, they say. So, I thought what I was trying to do is put in one place how I think and I worked in 2005. I was working sometimes four jobs. In 2004, I had been involved in the telecom, and you remember 2004 was not a good year and 2003 and 2002 weren't great either. I had also gotten involved in another business after that where I knew that in 2004 we were going to be in a crash, which we were. We lost everything. Lost the house we'd lived in for seventeen years, lost our cars, lost everything, which was frankly an answered prayer.

MacKenzie, who was the main character in the book, spends a weekend in the shack. That weekend represents eleven years of my life. The last year of those eleven years was 2004, and the last big fear I was trying to deal with was the fear of financial insecurity. Well, there's nothing like losing everything to help you deal with the fear of financial insecurity, let me tell you.

So, in 2005, we're living in a little tiny rental house in Gresham, Oregon, which is about 900 square feet of usable space. There are six of us in the house. I'm working three to four jobs. Kim has got a job two and a half blocks away at the local bakery at the high school, and we're about 150 feet away from the train station. That's why we had moved there because we couldn't afford the gas to get to the train station and so I could just walk over to the train, pick up, and go down to one of my jobs—my main job.

Well, I'm writing this story for my kids as I'm on the train, you know, forty minutes each way, and I start with the conversations. They start becoming living conversations for me, and I'm basically asking all the questions you're not allowed to ask when you're a kid growing up in the church, you know, in a religious environment. It took me about six months. People say, "How long did it take you to write the book?" I say, "Fifty years" because, in a sense that's true. The first manuscript was done in six months.

Now, that Christmas, we had nothing, and my goal was to get this done for Christmas and give it to my six kids and some of my friends. I got it done, but we didn't have any money.

Now here's a cool story: The book came out, and it has been this unbelievable phenomenon and it really is. It's now in the top, I think, fifty books of all time, in terms of sales. It's in forty-one languages and growing. It's unbelievable. I made fifteen copies at Office Depot and went back to work. But one of the countries that the book has done incredibly well (in) is Germany.

Tony: Let's fast-forward here a little bit because you get this book out and I had no clue the story behind your story and again, I want to thank you again . . . Let's talk about some of the challenges you had initially releasing the book. You just alluded to the fact you had a secular publisher, not a Christian based. How did the book break? What sort of initial momentum took off that floored you and your entire family.

Paul: Well, here's what happened: My friends kept giving it away. You know, you give your kids a book for Christmas, and then it's like, "Thanks, Dad. We'll get right on that." You know? So, it took them awhile. But my friends were all over it, and I get these calls. I was working at that time for a guy who's a friend of mine named Mike and so I get calls and my friends would go, "Hey. We have friends or I have a friend who I really would like to give this book (to) . . . would that be okay?" You have to understand. I went to Office Depot, it's a little spiral-bound, photocopied plastic sheet cover on the front that says, "*The Shack* by MacKenzie Allen Phillips, who's the main character, and M.P. Young," which was a joke, you know for my kids.

Tony: Love it.

Paul: Well, two funny things happened because of that; one is because of my friends, I had to make fifteen more copies at Office

Depot so they could give them away, and then pretty soon I'm getting emails from people I don't know who want to come to Portland and have lunch with MacKenzie because he wrote this book and that's the problem. The other funny thing is that nobody in my world knows me as William. My dad is William Henry. I'm William Paul. My son is William Chad. My grandson is William Gab, and we all go by our middle names. Nobody knows me as William, and when the book eventually got published for real, I'd have people call me up and go, "Paul, have you read this book by this William Young? He thinks just like you," you know, which was great.

Tony: Paul, really quick, for our global audience. My hair is standing at the back of my neck because I'm a marketing guy. You know, I teach all over the world. I've written a few books, and I know the complexities of getting in-store placement and product display. I want to let our audience know a few instructive things you just said. You didn't spend much money because the book is not only phenomenal, but word-of-mouth marketing is the most effective form ever created. You go back to any historical time, you know, Jesus started out with twelve disciples that told the story and look where they ended up. So that alone should tell our audience, "Aha! Well I can't do this or I can't do that. I don't have any money. I can't afford. I don't have any investor's." Your entire story is so gripping because you made things happen that most would say there's just no way and you kept rebuilding and reinvesting your profits and all of a sudden good things happen because of word of mouth.

Paul: Don't look at me. I mean, you know what, I think God has a great sense of humor. I understand everything you're saying, but there's a piece to this that is far more important because success is not defined as bottom line. Success is not even defined by outcome. Success is defined by who you are as a human being and what happens in this process. I'd much rather a person come through a fire and come out the other side a more healed human being than a rich one in a monetary sense.

You know, back in 2005 when I was writing this story for my kids, my prayer was this: It was . . . and Papa is my name for God the Father . . . and it's, you know, *Papa, I'm never going to ask you again to bless anything that I do.* Now, that's half the prayer. And that half, let me explain it a little bit, that is I'm a religious kid. I grew up in a religious environment. I was as good a Pharisee as anybody, and it was all performance. That was my image of God, and I was trying to win the approval and the affection of God, just like I've been trying to my whole life with my own father.

Tony: I want to dig into the interior of the book. This is an actual quote from Dale Lang, who is the father of one of the students that was killed in the Columbine shooting . . . "*The Shack* goes beyond being the well-written suspenseful page turner that it is. Since the death of our son, Jason, the Lord has led us to a small number of life-changing books and this one heads the list. When you close the back cover, you will be changed."

Paul, you've got all sorts of celebrities to everyday people that have experienced tragedy and triumph that have endorsed the book, and I'm tempted not to talk about the story because I want people to get into it and go, "Oh my goodness. I can't put the thing down." But I want to go into it a little bit if we can. Kind of tease our audience because our audience will buy a book, so you might have a spike on Amazon here shortly. But let's talk about, you know, an overview. The main character in the book, his name is Mack and he has a tragedy that befalls him. If you could kind of take us through in a couple of minutes because I have some other great questions, and I want to be very respectful of your time. What happens to Mack, and how did you come up with his storyline to take us into *The Shack*?

Paul: Okay. The book is based in great tragedy and to me, the deepest pain a human being can experience is the loss between a parent and a child. This is the centerpiece. And people say, "How can you write a book like this for your own children?" And my response is, "You know, I didn't think about other scenarios like a great illness or something, but there was nothing that touches the deep places like this does." I said, "You know what. It's the deepest pain, and the deepest pain asks the best questions."

So, I'm writing this for my kids thinking, *Okay, this asks the right questions.* A writer from Nashville, she wrote me after the book . . . first came out, and she said, "You know, I don't know your history or your back story, but my sense is that Missy, who's the main character's daughter, that Missy represents something murdered in you as a child, probably your innocence, and MacKenzie is you as an adult trying to deal with that." I showed that to Kim, and she said, "Boy, she nailed it." I mean, we've had the deaths in our own family. We've known some of that, and we had a six-month period, Kim lost her mom at fifty-nine, but three months before, my eighteen-year-old brother was killed and three months after, my five-year-old niece was killed the day after her fifth birthday. So, we know about some of that, but this also goes into the losses that we as human beings experience.

And so MacKenzie, he goes camping with his kids in Eastern Oregon. It's a place that we've camped at and been to and his youngest daughter is abducted and there's evidence found at a shack, just a hunter's cabin way out in the reserve, that she may have been murdered, but they don't find her body and he's absolutely devastated.

He goes into what I call the great sadness, and amid this great sadness, a few years after the loss, he gets this mysterious note in the mailbox in the middle of an ice storm inviting him back to the shack; and the invitation is written in such a way that it potentially could be the perpetrator, it could be a horrendously bad joke and (in) poor taste. It could be even an invitation by God, and this whole situation has placed his relationship with God, his relationship even with his members of his family at risk, and so he goes back in order to see what this is really all about and goes back to the place of his greatest pain, and that's where everything else unfolds (in) the rest of the book.

Tony: Well, Paul, I mean there's something interesting, and a lot of my newsletter audience knows this, you talk about the great tragedy. MacKenzie's big issue with his daughter being abducted and you know, since I read it the first time until recently, you ask anyone of my personal spirit influence (friends) and many business associates, I've gone through the great year. The last twelve months have been like ten years of chaos put into one involving family and business. When you opened up the interview about thirty minutes ago telling everybody what you went through, I'm stunned, because no one would assume that this book that breaks would have such a fascinating miraculous backdrop, and it leads me right into this question: How has your life changed? I mean, you and your family and your six kids. I mean, you were literally on the brink. You're doing everything you could. You write this book. You photocopied), handed it out, and all of a sudden two to three years later, you can't script this. I mean, what is the biggest blessing you've seen or the biggest change, I should say?

Paul: Um, wow. Let me answer the question flat-out first and then, let me answer it this way. Part of the beauty of what has happened is that nothing that matters to me has changed. Everything that matters to me was in place before I wrote the book. And the book was really written out of (the) healing process and not part of one, and that has made a huge difference. So, the things that matter to me have just become more deeply precious. There's a lot of things that have happened that, you know, you just go *how cool is this, how fun, but if it all went away tomorrow, I'd be fine.* I was back cleaning toilets and shipping out soldering tips, which was my main job three and a half years ago. If I was doing that tomorrow, I'd be fine because the things that matter to me were already in place.

The most precious thing outside of all of that, people ask me what I do now that I don't clean toilets and ship soldering tips, you know, and I tell them, "I get to hang around burning bushes all day," and I love that because people—I mean, I've gotten over a hundred thousand, well over a hundred thousand emails and letters from all over the world about people telling me these unbelievable stories (about) how the book has intercepted into their processes, in their pain, in their hurt, and how it has transformed their view of themselves, of the character and nature of God. It comes from every kind of background—religious, nonreligious—it doesn't seem to matter.

Tony: . . . Why do you think, Paul—and I'm going to give you the floor on this one because the book really beautifully lays it out—why is forgiveness such a powerful act of healing that so many people refuse to accept or even practice?

Paul: It's because we have to let go of control. Forgiveness is really a fundamental letting go of control. Unforgiveness is primarily a prison that we find ourselves locked in, that other people may have helped us build, but then we find our sense of identity and worth or our sense of purpose and meaning inside that prison, and to let it down, you know, is a very hard thing for us and yet, it's so fundamental.

Tony: With the holiday season upon us, by the time this gets to our subscribers, (it) would be around Christmastime or New Year's. What advice or wisdom would you draw to share with our listeners who may get this and pass (it) along for 2012? What is your advice to make it your best year ever, to appreciate each day that you draw from *The Shack* and the stories that you hear?

Paul: Stay inside the grace of just one day. Let me explain that. At the beginning of 2005, this inexplicable thing happened. Joy showed up in my life as a constant companion rather than an occasional acquaintance, and I couldn't figure out why. I didn't pray for it. I wasn't looking for it. I didn't expect it. I didn't know it was possible, and suddenly joy had become a constant companion, and I'm thinking, *what is going on here?*

Six months into this, I'm talking to a friend of mine, and he asked me, "What happened at the beginning of 2005?" And I'm thinking about it, and I realized, *Oh yeah, I finally got to the place where I was healthy enough, that I was staying inside the grace of one day.* That is, most of my life, I've been projecting myself into imaginary futures—almost all are negative, destructive, horrific, whatever, you know. What if I lose this job? Or what if I don't get this promotion? What if I lose this sale? What if I . . . What if this happens to my kids? What if I get this disease, and what are they going to say at my funeral?

And what I was doing is I was spending today's grace because you only get grace for one day. Spending it on things that don't even exist, things that were freaking me out because I'm not God, and when I looked in those imaginations, God wasn't in them because God doesn't live in anything that's not real, and so it always pushed me back to control, and I would spend today's grace trying to control things that don't even exist. So, my encouragement is, as best as you know how, learn to stay inside the grace of just one day. Everything else is an imagination. I don't even know if I'll be here tomorrow. I could be driving over to, you know, the grocery store and some truck could take me out, you know.

Five Key "Mind Nuggets" from Paul to Ponder and Reflect Upon

1. *"Success is not even defined by outcome. Success is defined by who you are as a human being and what happens in this process. I'd much rather a person come through a fire and come out the other side a more healed human being than a rich one in a monetary sense."*

2. *"We lost everything. Lost the house we've lived in for seventeen years, lost our cars, lost everything, which was frankly an answered prayer.*

MacKenzie, who was the main character in the book, spends a weekend in the shack. That weekend represents eleven years of my life. In the last year of those eleven years was 2004, and the last big fear I was trying to deal with was the fear of financial insecurity."

3. *"The most precious thing outside of all of that, people ask me what I do now that I don't clean toilets and ship soldering tips, you know, and I tell them, "I get to hang around burning bushes all day," and I love that because people—I mean, I've gotten over a hundred thousand, well over a hundred thousand emails and letters from all over the world about people telling me these unbelievable stories.*

4. *"Forgiveness is really a fundamental letting go of control. Unforgiveness is primarily a prison that we find ourselves locked in, that other people may have helped us build, but then we find our sense of identity and worth or our sense of purpose and meaning inside that prison, and to let it down, you know, is a very hard thing for us and yet, it's so fundamental."*

5. *"So my encouragement is, as best as you know how, learn to stay inside the grace of just one day. Everything else is an imagination. I don't even know if I'll be here tomorrow. I could be driving over to, you know, the grocery store and some truck could take me out, you know."*

What Else Paul Revealed During our Interview

Here are a few more of the areas we discussed during our *Captured Wisdom* audio interview, which can be accessed at www.mindcapturebook.com/ interviews:

*   *The amazing story of how the book started out as fifteen copies for close friends and family and then picked up momentum by spreading like wildfire via amazing word-of-mouth sales*

- *How miracles or "God winks" are always around us and how to spot them*
- *Why storytelling is the most effective way to share any message*
- *The stunning story of how the book was published and marketed for less than $300*
- *How small acts of kindness can change the world for the better*
- *The power of forgiveness and the amazing story of a helicopter medic and her dying father*
- *Fifty-seven powerful takeaways that an atheist had after reading the book*
- *Why each day is a gift and how to make the most of the present moment*

About Spirit Trailblazer, Wm Paul Young

William P. Young was born a Canadian and raised among a stone-age tribe by his missionary parents in the highlands of what was New Guinea. He suffered great loss as a child and young adult, and now enjoys the 'wastefulness of grace' with his family in the Pacific Northwest.

Young had written primarily as a way to create unique gifts for his friends, until his wife repeatedly urged him to write something for their six children in order to put down in one place his perspectives on God and on the inner healing Young had experienced as an adult. The resulting manuscript, that later became The Shack, was intended only for his six kids and for a handful of close friends.

Young initially printed just 15 copies of his book. Two of his close friends encouraged him to have it published and assisted with some editing and rewriting in order to prepare the manuscript for publication. Rejected by 26 publishers, Young and his friends published the book under the name of their newly created publishing company, Windblown Media in 2007.

The company spent only $200 in advertising. Word-of-mouth referrals eventually drove the book to number one on the New York Times trade paperback fiction best-seller list. In June 2008 The Shack" was the top-selling fiction and audio book of 2008 in America through November 30.

For more information visit:

wmpaulyoung.com

CHAPTER 4
JOHN STOSSEL

"I was the odd duck at ABC. I came in as a normal duck, another liberal who loves regulation and thought it was the solution to problems, and woke up, finally, to the fact that regulation does more harm than good. I started trying to do stories on the benefits of individual freedom and limits at government and capitalism and was despised by some people there."

—John Stossel

Free-Thinking Trailblazer

I've been a fan of John Stossel's work for twenty-plus years and here's why: He cuts to the chase, through the BS, and asks the tough questions that a good journalist is trained and supposed to ask. For example, when opinion polls show a record low vote of confidence in our elected officials in Washington, he continues to challenge government in a way that every American should be thankful for and appreciate. Instead of tuning government out, he turns up the heat to ask why we should put up with and tolerate such dissatisfaction.

Growing up watching Stossel sitting next to Barbara Walters and the late Hugh Downs on ABC's classic show *20/20* every Friday night, I found his unique consumer-related stories and personality to be entertaining and thought provoking.

When I came across his book *No, They Can't: Why Government Fails-But Individuals Succeed,* I made a note to not only pick up a copy, but also to reach out to his team about a possible interview. With an audience of ten million viewers per week on his FOX-TV show, I knew the challenge would be not so much getting an interview (Yes, I think BIG!), but more likely finding the right PR people to reach out and get my media request in front of and reviewed for consideration.

Instead of feeling defeated by the thought of finding, yet alone, getting his PR people on the phone, I quickly thought, *I wonder if he's doing a media tour or any book signings.* This little hunch then prompted me to do a quick Google search and then find a listing for a book event in Florida at a Barnes & Noble store that he'd soon be appearing at. Next, I called the store, got the manager on the line after being on hold a few minutes, told them my request, and was then given a name in New York City at corporate. I immediately called that person and left a descriptive message and my cell number.

The next day, a call came in from Barnes & Noble in New York with a name and number to call at John's publisher. I called, left a voicemail message, and the next day I got a call back. I quickly explained my request, and no joke, two days later I got an email confirming a greenlight for the interview. I mention all this because it once again demonstrates that persistence, asking questions, and doing your homework often pay off.

The three main things I enjoyed most about my interview with John include:

1. He's very much into personal responsibility and freedom, which is a tough sell in today's mainstream media structure that packages and sells entitlements up and down the dial.
2. He makes you really think about how much regulation is taking place in our lives and the many unintended consequences it brings when it's left unchecked.
3. He displays a willingness to question and report on the many abuses and rabid waste taking place within the federal government at a time when the US can ill afford to take on more debt.

Key Highlights from Our Interview

Tony: Excellent. John, I want to come out, because I know your time is very, very valuable, and open up with really a quick question that's pretty simple to set the tone: Why did you write this book at this moment in time?

John: Because the government keeps screwing up and going off the cliff . . . reality has taught me that government makes problems worse, and I wanted to share what I've learned.

Tony: Interesting. John, it takes me to my next question here. I was a fan of yours for probably twenty years when you were on ABC's *20/20*. I always thought—I'm 39, John—watching you in my twenties that you seemed kind of like the odd duck at ABC. Explain the difference of now working with Fox and really the differences between ABC and Fox and how you feel somewhat more liberated like you talk about in the book.

John: I was the odd duck at ABC. I came in as a normal duck, another liberal who loves regulation and thought it was the solution to problems, and woke up, finally, (to the fact) that regulation does more harm than good. (I) started trying to do stories on the benefits of individual freedom and limits at government and capitalism and was despised by some people there.

Peter Jennings would jerk his head and look away when he would see me in the hall because in his mind I had betrayed the objectivity of ABC News. Everybody in the building was down the middle objective, and the only guy with an opinion was me.

Tony: Well, John, you look at that when you're on television. I could swear some nights Barbara Walters wanted to smack you. Did you ever sense that in the studio? She's a great interviewer, but I could sense that for years. I'm like, "How is Stossel making it on ABC?"

John: She was actually one of the more open-minded, smart, and sympathetic people. She even once said to another correspondent, "You can't have a law for everything." But yeah, she looks at me as that odd duck, that odd libertarian. And eventually they stopped putting my stories on, and I got so frustrated that I—I wasn't recruited by Fox. I called Fox and begged for a job.

Tony: Well, this is interesting to me because I know that as in marketing, a lot of our audience is entrepreneurs, CEOs—I teach marketing, John. I remember the tagline, "Give me a break." That stuck in my head for twenty years. I have to give you credit for branding me. We go into more of your great book here . . .

John, let's keep moving here. This is such a great book. You say again, "What intuition tempts us to believe, some institutions are too big to fail. What reality taught me, failure makes markets work?" John, why are bailouts a bad thing in your opinion?

John: Because they create more hazards. They say you can take risks and often with other people's money, and nothing's at risk. So, you take some risks. And the beauty of market discipline is that it works better than all the written regulations. After Enron blew up, Sarbanes–Oxley was promised to make sure it never happened again. But of course, then came the housing bubble and the deceitful mortgages and Bernie Madoff. There were laws preventing against all that stuff. But the laws are so complex, nobody really understands them.

The laws give investors a false sense of security so that they think they're protected by government. And that leads some of them to give all their money to the Bernie Madoffs of the world. We're much better off that things can fail. Spread your money around, check things out yourself, or hire people that have a record of evaluating investments, and don't rely on any one institution, including government, as security.

Tony: We go on to chapter nine a little bit here about educating children. I'll give you sort of what reality taught you. You said that government schools are one of the worst parts of America. Wow! Give us your thoughts on that. That's a pretty bold statement.

John: We're intrinsic to believe that public schools are one of the best parts about America, the great melting pot. But in fact, they are a government monopoly. And like all government monopolies, they don't serve their customers very well. So first a melting pot. It turns out that the way people evade the melting pot is to move to different neighborhoods, to be assigned to different schools. And public schools are now more segregated than private schools.

And public-school students are more likely to sit in a single race group in the lunchroom than in private school. I shouldn't call them public and private schools because what's public about public schools? Can you walk into your kid's public school? No. A private supermarket is open and much more accessible to the public. Let's just call them government schools. They're government funded, and like all government-run things, they're bad.

Now they say they don't fund them well enough. Well, they fund them unbelievably well. We're spending today $12,000 per student. Do the math. That's more than $200,000, almost $300,000 per classroom. Think what you could do with that money. You could hire great teachers. But where does the money go? We don't know. Money just disappears in government monopolies. They're not spending it on gross things like the Las Vegas run by the GSA. They're wasting it hiring assistants to the assistants to the assistant principal and having silly speech code classes and being politically correct.

But everything has improved in America in the last thirty years—cars, phones. But schools are the same. Why? Because there's no competition. Because you're assigned to your school based on where you live.

Imagine if we bought groceries in the same way and you were assigned to your neighborhood grocery store. There would be no competition there, and the groceries would be like groceries in the Soviet Union. The shelves would be largely bare.

Tony: Yeah. Well you go back to the elephant in the room, the US debt, John. This seems to be never-ending. You give some great ideas in the book of other countries that have dealt with the debt issue. You talk about Canada. What did Canada do that seems to have worked so well that maybe we could wake up and have a sober pill and say, "Look, we've got to look at what Canada did?" Explain.

John: In the '90s, Canada was on a track much like ours. Spending was going up, and they saw they were making promises to people, for example, that they couldn't keep. There wouldn't be enough young people to pay for it, and so they cut spending sharply. And not straight cuts like we do in the United States. We're going to cut 20 percent when they really need. We've got to cut 20 percent for what they wish they could spend next year and still make an increase. These were actual cuts.

The reforms were made by a liberal government. It saw what the future was, and perhaps they were easier to make because they came from liberals. But the result was they shrank government. They also increased taxes, but the cut was six-to-one for the tax increases. And today the Canadian dollar is worth an American dollar. And Canada is doing quite well. They also had no Fannie and Freddie and federal housing administration. And they have a higher home ownership rate than the United States. And they had no housing bubble.

Tony: Well, I noticed that too, John. In the late '90s when we went to Toronto, my family, the exchange rate was much more favorably tilted to the US. And now the Canadians are coming down. Michigan is home for me sometimes, and I'm out in the northwest and they come down from the border because the exchange rate now favors the Canadians.

John: Yeah, let's go to the third world country of the United States and buy stuff. The dollar is worthless.

Tony: Interesting.

John: And that's going to get worse as the American government prints more money to pay for my Medicare bills.

Tony: . . . Folks, go out and get this (Stossel's) book. I'm going to warn you, if you're like me it's going to be highlighted and dog-eared. This is a phenomenal book, very timely. And, John, any other quick thoughts before we wrap up our time? I really appreciate you with the busy schedule you have on TV and radio. Some other quick thoughts about the book and what you're seeing out there or the reaction with the book?

John: This is the first week of the book tour. People love it. But of course, I'm speaking to people who would attend to all of these ideas. Who knows what other people think? Government fails, but individuals succeed. We need to learn this because as Thomas Jefferson said, it's the natural progress of things for government to grow. It's growing from 1 percent of GDP to 40 percent of GDP. We can't keep this up. We don't have to make all the cuts I made in chapter thirteen, but we need to make many for us to have a future.

Tony: And ironically, John, it could not escape that (in) chapter thirteen you talked about cuts, the reference there. John Stossel, let me read one final thing here near the end of the book, and then I will thank you for your time. You say here near the end, "There is nothing that government can do that we cannot do better as free individuals. And as groups of individuals, working together voluntarily, not at the point of gun or under threat of a fine. Without big government, our possibilities are limitless." John Stossel, I commend you. Congratulations on this, and keep up the good work you're doing.

John: Thank you, Tony.

Five Key "Mind Nuggets" from John to Ponder and Reflect Upon

1. *After four decades of reporting, I've finally figured out that to think that government can solve problems and reality has taught me that government makes problems worse and I wanted to share what I learned."*

2. *"But everything has improved in America in the last thirty years— cars, phones. But schools are the same. Why? Because there's no competition. Because you're assigned to your school based on where you live."*

3. *"She (Barbara Walters) was actually one of the more open-minded, smart, and sympathetic people. She even once said to another correspondent, 'You can't have a law for everything.' But yeah, she looks at me as like that odd duck, that odd libertarian. And eventually they stopped putting my stories on, and I got so frustrated that I—I wasn't recruited by FOX. I called FOX and begged for a job."*

4. *"So better to leave money in private hands as much as possible. We need the government for personal security. We need police forces. That's not the federal government. That's state and local. We need the government for defense. But we don't need to spend nearly four trillion dollars when we're going broke."*

5. *"No one should be trusted to tell somebody else to shut up. Color of Change wants me to shut up because I say two parts of the Civil Rights Act, two parts of the seven, are unconstitutional in my opinion. Those are the parts that forbid private discrimination. Civil Rights acts were a good thing because they ended government*

discrimination. They ended Jim Crow. They ended forced segregation in places that forced blacks to use a different drinking fountain. Government should never discriminate against anybody."

What Else John Revealed During Our Interview

Here are a few more of the areas we discussed during our *Captured Wisdom* audio interview, which can be accessed at www.mindcapturebook.com/interviews:

- *Why the government must be questioned and continually investigated*
- *How laws designed to protect and help people often have negative, unintended consequences*
- *The power of sticking to your convictions even in the face of intense opposition and criticism*
- *Why corporate bailouts are a bad thing*
- *Why genuine capitalism is a good thing*
- *The glaring hypocrisy in most laws and why free speech is so important*
- *Why banning certain things oftentimes backfires and makes the item even more desirable*
- *The negative effect that high taxes have on people and their motivation to work more or less*

About Free Thinking Trailblazer, John Stossel

John Stossel joined Fox Business Network (FBN) in 2009. He is the host of "Stossel", a weekly program highlighting current consumer issues with a libertarian viewpoint. Stossel also appears regularly on Fox News Channel (FNC) providing signature analysis.

Prior to joining FBN, Stossel co-anchored ABC's primetime newsmagazine show, "20/20." There, he contributed in-depth special reports and recurring segments on a variety of consumer topics, from pop culture to government and business. His "John Stossel specials" asked tough questions facing Americans today: "Sick in America" delved into the debate between private vs. government health care; "Stupid in America" exposed the government school monopoly; "John Stossel Goes to Washington" revealed government growth under both parties, while "Hype" exposed media distortions.

Stossel's economic programs have been adapted into teaching kits by a non-profit organization, "Stossel in the Classroom." High school teachers in American public schools now use the videos to help educate their students on economics and economic freedom. They are seen by more than 12 million students every year. Stossel has received 19 Emmy Awards and has been honored five times for excellence in consumer reporting by the National Press Club.

For more information visit:
Johnstossel.com

CHAPTER 5

DAN BYLSMA

"I think the best thing a leader can do is use specific words, have a specific vision, so when you say things, everybody has the same picture in their brain."

—Dan Bylsma

Belief Trailblazer

It's amazing to get into the mind of a person to discover what really makes them tick, especially when it's related to how they get others to perform at a very high level. When I was given the chance to interview the head coach of the NHL's Pittsburgh Penguins, Dan Bylsma, I was excited for a variety of reasons, but the main one being that he'd just come off winning the Stanley Cup, hockey's most coveted trophy, a couple months earlier. Not only is winning this trophy extremely hard to do, but he also did it in his first year as head coach of the team!

As a huge hockey fan, this interview was not only fun, but I was also fortunate to ask Dan detailed questions regarding the mindset and what strategies he employed with the players to take them from a group that was clearly underperforming, to five months later becoming Stanley Cup champions.

Another huge thing that jumped out during our interview was Dan's humble nature. I've known Dan for many, many years, and not only is he a good coach, but he's also a very nice guy. For example, when we played on our church softball team in his summers when he was on break from playing NHL hockey, I found him to be a nice guy that you'd never even suspect was playing with the likes of Wayne Gretzky as a teammate in his full-time profession.

The three main things I enjoyed most about my interview with Dan include:

1. He shared a detailed look at how leaders work with the situation and mold it to their liking to produce a desired result.

2. He shared the simply stunning story about what he told his team before the Game 7 finals of the Stanley Cup championship against the Detroit Red Wings. I was thankful to God that we were taping the interview, especially this part, as what he shared with me was simply incredible.

3. Dan is living proof that if you work hard, focus on your strengths, and have a positive mindset, anything is possible. Sure, you don't get to the highest level of hockey, the NHL, without talent, but his ability to hustle, train relentlessly, and focus on the end goal were major reasons he made it to "The Show" and played for many years at the highest level.

Key Highlights from Our Interview

Tony: I appreciate you being on (the) line. We're going to talk about hockey, of course. Also, I want to talk about your publishing and maybe your hockey camp if we have time, but more importantly, the success mindset of a champion. Frankly, like I just said, what you guys pulled off, I've got to think, you're still pinching yourself.

Dan: [Chuckles] I still have a bruise on my left arm from where walking home from Mellon Arena to the hotel, where I stayed at for five months, just daily, and the pinch got harder and harder as we went into the playoffs, into the finals, and then winning. You just have to sometimes take a step back, and shake your head, and pinch yourself to check reality and you know, who you are, where you came from, and exactly what you're in the midst of doing. It was a fantastic thing, but people look at me in a new light, but I still look in the mirror and see, you know, the kid who grew up in Ellsworth from West Michigan. And looking in the mirror, I see my family, I see my wife and son, the important things to me, and not so much the guy who is wearing a suit on TV.

Tony: What do you think—turning the Penguins around was the turning point in the season? You guys (were) running in the eighth or ninth place when you took over . . . and ended) up winning the Stanley Cup. But what was the change in attitude that you think for that moment where you went, okay, we've got a shot here?

Dan: I think two things were key for us in changing what was happening prior to me getting there and then what happened after I got there. And one of them was, you know, the words you use in your life and the focus you have in your life kind of dictate how you get up in the morning a lot. It's your attitude that you bring into each day, and it's the things that motivate you and the thoughts that go into your brain that can push you down the road. Oh, they do push you down the road.

Some of those roads are good and some of them are bad roads, but we really, early on, had a meeting with the team and really it was the team talking, not the coaches talking.

We were guiding the process, but the process was who are we as a team? What do we think we can be? What will people think about us right now? Is that who we want to be? And if it's not, who do we want to be? Who can we be? And in some of the words that the players in the room described about what other teams think about us right now weren't good ones. They weren't ones that you like to hear about yourself and your team, and we were frank about them and we were . . . are they true? And a lot of them were true.

Who could we be and how could we play? And, you know, those words were energizing words. We can be fast, aggressive, or a skilled team. We can dictate. We can play in-your-face style of hockey, and we developed those words and we brought it down to five words or so. We gave it a name.

. . . and the credit goes to the players for really buying in and almost making this change immediately. Because of that, I think for a very short period of time the team started to understand exactly who they were going to play, exactly how it was going to look, and when you have that, you're starting to develop, you know, keep going in to Boston, and they're expecting a fast-skilled team that's going to play in your face and aggressive all night long, you have already won up on the scoreboard.

Tony: Now please tell me that you reminded them (the team) that you were in a Game 7 as a player, and you know, I think that maybe served to motivate them. What were their thoughts on that when you told them about your experience in Anaheim, you know, playing in the Game 7 Stanley Cup Final?

Dan: Well, I did certainly draw up on it. We had a few other players that were in the Game 7. One was Petr Sýkora and Ruslan Fedotenko, both guys who had played in the Game 7 for the Stanley Cup, and I think one of the, you know, one of the things that I learned about (in the) first time around in the finals in Game 7 and this time was . . . The first time around I thought . . . thoughts about the Stanley Cup, thoughts about what you do with the Cup if you won. Thoughts about winning were bad thoughts, try not to think about them. I was told not to think about them and push them off to the side and focus just on hockey. I know now that it's impossible not to do that. You know when you start getting to one game away from getting to the finals, you start to think about what the Stanley Cup is. The ring that you're going to possibly have a chance to get, the trophy, the Cup. All those things come into your mind. You do think about them. You think about them constantly, and to try to put them to the side, I think I actually wasted more energy, mental energy, entertaining those thoughts. So, I said to the players, "You're going to think about them, you think about them right now. Enjoy the thought. Let it be a motivating thought, what you'd do with the cup, the Stanley Cup ring. Getting your name on that trophy, being called a Stanley Cup champion, and think about them to motivate you and let them focus you, but then on game day it's time to be focused on hockey. But you can't not think about it, so I encourage the players to think about it. I encourage them to see what your Cup day would be like and even, you know, start to plant it in your head as to what that day might be like and use those thoughts as a motivating factor. That was one of the things I talked about. The other thing I talked about, I think initially when you talk about walking out onto the ice or going up to bat or getting that moment in the sun, you think it's a nervous moment. You get apprehensive about making a mistake or being hesitant about, you know, extending yourself. You don't want to do too much. I think that almost paralyzes a team or handicaps a team and how they play and how they should play.

I said to the guys on the day of Game 7, I asked the question to Billy Guerin, our most vocal and our most colorful guy in the dressing room.

I said, "Billy, how many Game 7s have you played in for the Stanley Cup?" And he said, "None." And I was shocked I caught Billy off guard a little bit. But I said, "None? You played in none?" I said, "I played in thousands and thousands of Game 7s in my backyard when I was a kid." You know, you got to chuckle about it, and everyone else nodded their head. Everyone has played that game. Everyone has played the Game 7.

Everyone is imagining Stanley Cup being out there in their backyard or in their basement or in their driveway and competing for it. The next question I asked was, "How many of you played well for the first hour, got the goal in those games when you were a kid, and you know almost every person has imagined themselves or been in the basement and won that Stanley Cup and scored a goal or made the save or blocked the shot. You all made the right play to win the Stanley Cup many, many, many times, and tonight is no different. This is our chance to finally do it, and the game will be on your stick. It will be . . . You will get to do it defensively or make the save. You've done it many times before, and this is our chance to finally go out and do it and really win the Stanley Cup." That was my approach for Game 7.

Tony: Wow. You know on that thought process, Dan, you've played with some of the greatest in the game. I mean, you came up to the LA Kings and you're trying to tell a funny story about playing with Wayne Gretzky. If we have time, we can cover that. Amongst the players you've played with, you're also an assistant captain with Anaheim for a couple of seasons. Who influenced you the most or really saved you a lot of time and grief when you made it to NHL?

Dan: Alright. I think, you know, I could tell a few different stories that had an impact on me and (I) kind of used as (a) guide for how you want to treat people and what you want to be and whatever you do. I made it to the NHL for a first full season, played there for a full year. I got sent down the following season at the beginning of the year, and after five games, I made my way back up to the team. I had played some good games, maybe ten—it was about ten games or so. Luc Robitaille, famous hockey player, one of the best all time left winger, goal score star in LA, came up to me in the dressing room after one of those games and just said, "What you're doing for the team, we need it, what you do in practice, what you do on the ice." He said, "You make us a better team when you are in the lineup."

As a guy who, you know, role player, certainly not at the level of Luc or the star players, trying to find a role, trying to find some permanency in the NHL and doing . . . or getting sent up or sent down, then he validated me as a player. He told me what I brought to the team and how it was a needed part of the team even though it was a small part or a role-player's part. He walked over to me, took two seconds of time, and said some modest words of what he believes, and he validated me as a player. He gave me the courage now to not worry about some of the other things you can't control, some of the things that are outside of your scope of work ethic and ability to have control on a day out and just bring what I brought to the team, and that act is something that I try to emulate thereafter as a player, making sure that people . . . say, "Hey, great job," "Hey, that was awesome." Giving people a life and a boost just by a few words. Also, at the same time, you know, here's a star guy. Here's a guy who has got many things also on his plate, and I was a younger kid. He didn't need to say it and he didn't need to take time, but he did and no matter how high you get or how low you get, that's a great lesson I learned from Luc, and I always say he's the best star player I ever played with in terms of the way he treated people.

Tony: That is awesome. You know, to give again our audience some perspective, I've had the pleasure to watch you play when you were in LA and in Anaheim, and I don't think a lot of people know but your role was reeling and help me out here, I'm describing my perspective as a fan. You were the grinder penalty kill champion. It's one of those inglorious roles in hockey, but it's essential in a tight game. You're always called on the penalty kill. You're legendary status, Dan, and it's on Wikipedia as well as blocking shots. Those pucks kept flying fast, and you were legendary for diving in front of them. You're pretty modest, but where do you get this insanity streak?

Dan: Well, it's out of more of a necessity than anything, but you know, as I was moving on to my career and trying to find, wanting to move up to more ice time and wanting to move up levels, and we all score goals and we all get points when we were younger, but as you get older, there's not that many Wayne Gretzky or Mario Lemieux's or Sidney Crosby's in the world, and you have to adapt your game and you have to find new avenues to succeed if you want to move up and you want to achieve some of your goals, and that was really coming out of college, at the end of my college career, that was something that started with me, penalty killing and blocking shots, and that's something you could do in practice while the skilled guys, while the good guys were playing the power play, you could get the attention of the coach and you could try to earn some playing time and earn some status in the team and that's where that started and it developed into really my role in what I did and it's really how I got to the NHL. If I continue to try to be a goal scorer like I was in high school and younger, I would have had a much shorter career and probably wouldn't have made it to the NHL, but that was my adaptation, that was my avenue, and that's something I developed and it became, as you said, the role player. That's what I brought to the team.

Tony: Let's change gears. What was the most trying point in your playing career? And you can draw from your youth experience. Maybe it's collegiately in Bowling Green or even the NHL. What was the point where you thought, *You know what, why am I doing this?* and how did you overcome that?

Dan: Well, you know, I think any road is easier to look back on and say, "Oh that's good, you know, how you played in the NHL for twelve years, and that's great, I wish I could have done that"; but as we all know, whatever road you're on, there are ups and downs and really a large portion of success is how you deal with those situations and the thoughts that go through your head and how motivated you are and how much you can stay focused on things that are important to you. I can, you know. I think of a couple different times that were keys for me and one of the ones that was a little bit later in my career as I've made the NHL for a year kind of surprised everybody. That I made a team at the NHL for the whole season and summer comes around again, and people were not that acquainted with the ins and outs of hockey and how contracts work and how many people are on the roster and how that works, so would now kind of talk to me about how I've made the NHL, and I was certainly going to be there and how was the year going to be next year in LA or Anaheim and that's not what I was feeling on the inside.

I was always feeling, well, I have to make the team, and I'm not sure that I'm going to do that. Those are the thoughts going through my brain and (I) often had to deal with, especially in the summertime, was what happens if I don't make the team? Am I failure? Are people going to look at me differently? Are the people now going to say he was just a one-hit wonder or he's a fluke?

And you go home and really start to worry about it when the lights go off or when you're privately in your own home. What does success mean to me? Do I have to make it to be successful? And, you know, the one thing that I left with the next morning . . . that was motivating to me is that my success has nothing to do with the level which I play at in terms of being in the NHL or the AHL. Am I working the appropriate way? Am I doing everything I can today? Am I doing everything I can this week to put myself in the best situation? I can be in to get what I want, you know, to achieve the goals that I want to achieve and that for me, at the end of the day, was how I laid my head on the pillow.

That is success for me. Did I do the right thing today? Am I aware of my strengths and weaknesses? Or am I trying to work towards getting better in those areas and underlining and emphasizing the strengths that I have? And am I doing that in a process where I can guarantee I'm going to be better next week and in the following week and in the next month because of my actions, because of my work ethic, because of my evaluation. And to me, and what I hung my head on, is that will be success for me regardless of what happens in my career.

Tony: How do you manage and motivate top talent? I know we hit on it the first part of the interview, but how do you parallel that with business? What clues do you give to our entrepreneurs, our business people on the call of managing top talent, that they could borrow from the game of hockey in your role as a head coach?

Dan: I think, you know, first of all as a coach. I'm not a treat-everyone-equally type of person. There are different people that you're going to deal with. I have Sidney Crosby. I have Max Talbot. I have Craig Adams. Everyone knows Sidney Crosby. Very few people would probably know the name Craig Adams, but they all deserve to be treated fairly, but they're not going to be treated equally. One person may be thirty-eight years old and another may be twenty. One may be playing a majority of the time on the ice, and one may not be playing very much at all and so different situations for different people. But, I do think that each person, they have pride, they have a work ethic. They have a want to do well, and they have a want to do better, and I really do believe that.

When all the people that I interact with, there are very few people that I have met that don't have those things and I mean, very few. And so, giving direction, being plain and communicating clearly about expectations, showing them what their foundation is, what they do well as individuals, what they need to work on but drawing out continuously an evaluation of that foundation on a daily basis—get them involved in that process. Show them the potential of where they can go and where our team can go on a situation and involving them in that process on a daily basis and holding them accountable through your evaluation, through their evaluation, and you really start to develop an atmosphere where people have a chance to do well and know how to do well, have the tools to do well, and that's an energizing and exciting thing to be a part of. And when you can build that excitement, when you can build that energy and passion in a player, in a person, in a team, in a business, you start to sow the seeds for them taking ownership, them being invested, the team, the people being invested and now, together you start going towards a clear goal, a clear vision. And you do it with passion and energy, and I'm getting excited right now just talking about it.

Tony: Well, again ladies and gentlemen, I want to thank Dan Bylsma, head coach of Pittsburgh Penguins, for a very fascinating, you know, I call it Confessions of the Cup interview about life, success, motivation, and really how to have incredible leadership. So, Dan, I look forward to seeing you. I'll try to get to a game in Pittsburgh this fall or maybe catch you guys up in Chicago. I want to thank you again for giving up an hour on a Saturday to do this before training camp breaks in a couple of weeks. And again, I wish you massive success except occasionally against my (Detroit) Wings, but I'll forgive you.

Dan: Yes. Thank you.

Tony: Thank you again, and have a great weekend.

Dan: I appreciate it. Thanks for the conversation, and you take care.

Five Key "Mind Nuggets" from Dan to Ponder and Reflect Upon

1. *"What would I say if I was Sidney Crosby's coach? I went in the next morning to talk to my boss and talk to the general manager and said, 'I've changed my mind. I'm not going to go in soft. I'm not going to go in testing the waters. I think this needs to be said. I think this is what I need to do, and I think it's important that I do it now.' . . . He said, 'I think you're right.'"*

2. *"I think two things were key for us in changing what was happening prior to me getting there and then what happened after I got there, and one of them was, you know, the words you use in your life and the focus you have in your life kind of dictate how you get up in the morning a lot. It's your attitude that you bring into each day, and it's the things that motivate you and the thoughts that go into your brain that can push you down the road."*

3. *"I said to the guys on the day of Game 7, I asked the question to Billy Guerin, our most vocal and our most colorful guy in the dressing room. I said, "Billy, how many Game 7s have you played in for the Stanley Cup?" And he said, "None." And I was shocked I caught Billy off guard a little bit. But I said, "None? You played in none?" I said, "I played in thousands and thousands of Game 7s in my backyard when I was a kid." You know, you got to chuckle about it, and everyone else nodded their head. Everyone has played that game. Everyone has played the Game 7."*

4. *"I think any road is easier to look back on and say, 'Oh that's good, you know, how you played in the NHL for twelve years, and that's great, I wish I could have done that'; but as we all know, whatever road you're in, there are ups and downs, and really a large portion of success is how you deal with those situations and the thoughts that go through your head and how motivated you are and how much you can stay focused on things that are important to you."*

5. *"I still now like to work on my skills because that's enjoyable to me. I'm passionate about that, and when you bring that passion, when you bring that excitement, when you bring that to what you do, then the work melts away and the hours melt away."*

What Else Dan Revealed During Our Interview

Here are a few more of the areas we discussed during our *Captured Wisdom* audio interview, which can be accessed at www.mincapturebook.com/interviews:

- *What it's really like to coach at the highest level of sports*
- *How to lead a team when every move is scrutinized and appears on TV for the world to see*
- *How passion, focus, and being coachable can lead to incredible success in sports, life, and business*
- *Why vision and attitude are important in achieving goals*
- *The power of mentorship and having positive role models in life who believe in you*
- *Why continuous improvement is essential in any profession*

About Belief Trailblazer, Dan Bylsma

Dan Bylsma is a leader and former head coach of the Pittsburgh Penguins. In his first year as head coach of the team in 2009 he led the team to a Stanley Cup championship, winning the Jack Adams Award as the NHL's "Most Outstanding Coach," and an Atlantic Division title in just five-plus seasons behind the bench.

He oversaw one of the most dramatic playoff runs in NHL history. The Penguins clinched all four series on the road, twice rallying from 2-0 series deficits (against Washington and Detroit). Pittsburgh beat the defending champion Red Wings four times in the last five games to claim the Cup, including a 2-1 Game 7 victory in Detroit.

Bylsma became the 14th rookie head coach, and just the fourth in the past 50 years, to capture the Stanley Cup. Of those 14, only Montreal's Al MacNeil took over mid-season (1970-71).

The Grand Haven, Michigan native realized one of his life-long dreams by representing his country at the 2014 Winter Olympics Games in Sochi, Russia as head coach of Team USA.

Bylsma led the Penguins to three 100-point seasons and five consecutive playoff berths, while becoming the winningest playoff coach in team history with 36 postseason victories and seven playoff series victories. Bylsma has the best regular-season winning percentage (.669) in team history with an all-time record of 201-93-25. His 201 wins are the second most in team history (Eddie Johnston, 232). He became the fastest coach in NHL history to reach 200 wins (316 games) in a 3-1 victory at Ottawa April 22, 2013.

He served as the head coach of the Buffalo Sabres through 2017 and is now a studio analyst with the NHL Network.

CHAPTER 6

JOEL COMM

Photo Credit: Anne Barbyte

"Live video is the most important revolution in social media since the advent of the smartphone. Some people don't quite see it that way yet, but they will."

—Joel Comm

Social Media Trailblazer

Way back in 2008 I was fortunate to meet Joel Comm at Book Expo America (BEA) in Los Angeles. I was gearing up promotions for my second book in the *Mind Capture* series, and I made it a point to make sure that Joel and I connected while at the convention. Let's just say we did, but I became a fan of Joel. We've stayed in touch since that fateful day in LA, and I've become an even bigger fan and promoter of his work for two main reasons:

1. He's typically spot-on at identifying online trends and relevant firms of value long before everyone else. Then he quickly shares with others online how and why they should consider using them.
2. He's a class act and genuinely nice guy.

That being said, as the years have passed, I've watched him successfully employ and use social media and excellent viral marketing to promote his own work. In addition, he's written several books on the topics of social media ranging from Google AdWords to Twitter and many other relevant business books geared toward successful entrepreneurship. He doesn't just write about online marketing and trends, he also uses them as well. This is a rare combination.

Social media can be a confusing and often controversial topic as people use it in a variety of ways. At the same time, it keeps changing almost weekly with new trends and players jumping into the online space. It's a shiny, short-attention-span place, and determining what sticks around and takes off and what social media tools and platforms will disappear is not an exact science. Joel has a great knack for picking up on what is worth examining and focusing on. This not only saves time but also shortens the learning curve for those who either read his books, attend his training or keynotes, or retain him privately for advice on this hot topic.

So, brace yourself for a real treat as we capture wisdom from not only one of the Internet pioneers, but also a very smart guy when it comes to making better sense of not just why social media can't be ignored, but, most importantly, how to manage and use it more effectively in your personal and professional life.

The three main things I enjoyed most about my interview with Joel include:

1. His sense of humor on what could be considered a serious topic. After the interview was rolling and I introduced him, he shifted from the key point of our interview focus to the importance of bacon. I'm not kidding!

2. He has a great ability to make the complex simple as it relates to how we view, use, and adapt to social media and its relevance. Social media is a very wide-open place, and he's good at identifying what tools are essential for any business and what to be on the lookout for as the next "big things."

3. He is a big fan of lifelong learning. He never gets comfortable with a trend and stops. His body of online work, writing, and continual use of social media each day proves it. His hunger and childlike curiosity when it comes to using the Internet the past twenty-two years, and now social media, to communicate, socialize, and successfully promote, makes him a unique and engaging thought leader.

Key Highlights from Our Interview

Tony: All right. Well, let's talk about right now. You and I had the opportunity to talk privately. No cameras rolling, no interview taping. What are you looking at right now as being a big trend in the digital space? I know it, but I'd love to hear your current real-time view. What is the big thing in social media and digital marketing?

Joel: Well, clearly, I don't say everybody is talking about it, but those who are watching are talking about (it) and clearly, the most important trend right now on social media is bacon. You're like, "Wait, that's not what I was expecting at all." No, humor aside and my little bacon joke there, live video is the most important revolution in social media since the advent of the smartphone. (. . .) Some people don't quite see it that way yet, but they will, the same way that those that you know when the smartphones came out, when we got the first iPhone in 2007. I had one of the first ones because I was like, "This is it. This is the game changer. This changes everything." And then several years go by and people looked back and go, "Wow, that smartphone changed everything. The way we get information. The way we engage. The way we interact." And live video is having that same effect right now, and it's just going to be more pervasive and more game-changing than anything we've seen and bacon.

Tony: I love it, and I'm a huge fan of both, not Kevin Bacon but the meat. I'm not a vegetarian so—

Joel: Well, I'm not a fan of Kevin Bacon. I mean, he is okay.

Tony: We've got to get him on an interview. We'll put him on one of your podcasts.

Joel: There you go.

Tony: You can tell the energy of this call. We like to have fun, and regardless of what's going on before, we might get on a phone call or our day is going, you know life is short and social media, those two words, a lot of people misunderstand it. When you get asked by companies of all shapes and sizes, "Hey, help us out (to) understand social media," what would you tell them as sort of an initial base point? Again, we have listeners all over the world. How do you describe social media, and what should I do first as far as getting this thing effectively going? What's the strategy you'd recommend to them?

Joel: Well, the social space is all about town hall. It's where people were gathering to have conversations. Facebook's got 1.5 billion members from all around the world. Twitter's got 300 million active users, and the numbers just go on from there. And this is where people are gathering now to talk about anything and everything, whether it's (a) broad topic that we can all relate to, like parenting or dog(s) or the news, or whether there's special interest groups that can be extremely micro niche, that's just any kind of vertical. This is where people are having the discussion, and if you're not involved, especially as a businessperson in social media with the present, then you're basically opting out of the most important discussions that are taking place with your customers, with your prospects, with your competition, and the general public. And as far as where to get started, the low-hanging fruit is certainly Facebook because it's where the widest audience is, and that's where you find the most variety in terms of being able to discover people with similar interests.

Tony: So, here's your next question. You've been on the web since its conception. How do you keep adapting, Joel? How do you stay excited about this with all this fast and furious change?

Joel: Well, and let me say this, as of this call today, my first website turns twenty-one in just a few days. The first domain I ever registered will be of legal age.

Tony: There you go.

Joel: Look, I am labeled a futurist, one of the many labels I carry, and I'm still not exactly sure what that means. I like to play, and I've always been fascinated by technology. I've had a computer since 1980. I've been dialing in to the online world since 1980, and for me, it's always been something that's just fascinated and intrigued me. So, when I see something that captures my attention, I go, "Oh, what's that? I want to play with that." And many times, having that curiosity, that nature of mine that just wants to explore and play with the coolest toys in the toy store, to see what's new and interesting.

Turns out, I've become proficient and a person that people then look to, to say, "Hey, how do you this?" And it happened again and again and again, and I don't think it's because I'm so particularly smart, because I really don't think I am. I think it's the curiosity and the willingness to take a risk and say, "Hey, what does this thing do, and how can I use it and how can I either have fun with it or teach something with it or inspire people with it?" And, as a result of that natural curiosity, it's put me on the front line again and again, and live videos (are) no exception. I was doing live video since 2008, when newstream.tv was one of the first ones on the playing field.

And then what happened, Tony, is we have this perfect storm take place in early 2015. We finally have mass mobile adaption, where most people have smartphones now. We finally have bandwidth, even on cellular networks that can support live-streaming video in most regions, and we have easy-to-use applications that are being designed now.

In early 2015, we saw the release of an app called Meerkat. Now, it wasn't the first live video app to hit the phones, but it was the first app that got attention and got widespread use and media attention. Right on the heels of that, we have an app called Periscope that was purchased by Twitter, that then got blown up in the media and people were using it *en masse*. Because now this perfect storm of having the phone, having the bandwidth, and having the easy-to-use app all of a sudden is what put people everywhere, in front of the camera so they could instantly go live to the world, to reach an audience with their message, with their knowledge, with their whatever inspiration, and in whichever form of entertainment they wanted to deliver. And, the world changed.

And so now, what we're seeing is that the big boys and the little competitors are coming out. We have Facebook Live, we have YouTube Live, and soon an app for YouTube. We have the Musical.ly app, which is huge with children . . . and there's so many more. My phone is absolutely filled with live video options and my PC, by going on the web, there's all kinds of live video options. So, it's the Wild West in the live-video niche now.

Tony: So again, let's talk about video. Why do you think it's being so heavily marketed by Facebook and Twitter, and how do you think it is going to shake out? Who will be the winners? If you could give some predictions here.

Joel: Well, we are a very visual culture now since television took over radio. Radio still exists and print still exists, but since then, eyeballs were commanded by TV. Traditionally, TV has owned those eyeballs when we're talking first about the major networks, the big three, then, some local channels and then, we've got cable channels now. Then along comes Netflix and Hulu and Amazon Prime, giving people what they want, when they want it. They've been trained for that, right? To know hey, I want to watch this and I want to now and I want to binge watch this show. I don't want to wait for another season, so on, and so forth.

And we've been trained to get what we want, when we want. Well, now along comes the ability for anybody to broadcast, and people can consume what they want, when they want through live video. The big players are the usual suspects: Facebook, YouTube, Twitter, but there's going to be more coming on the scene. It wouldn't surprise me if Snapchat came up with a live video component. It wouldn't surprise me for Amazon and Netflix to develop an application and a tool for people to create original content that could be broadcast both live or archived on their services. Microsoft recently purchased LinkedIn. I think that there's a perfect opportunity using the Microsoft Skype technology to create a live video channel for businesses that would go through LinkedIn.

So, a lot of opportunities and clearly Facebook is going to be a major player because they have more eyeballs than anybody, and Mark Zuckerberg has told us that this is a prime initiative and they believe that video is going to count for a large percentage of the content that is shared over Facebook in the future.

Tony: Let's talk about mentors for a minute. Who were some people—I want to take a guess, maybe Bryan Kramer and Chris Brogan—but who are a couple of people that might surprise the fans of Joel Comm, that have influenced you that may be alive or dead, or maybe it's a printed book that has really changed your career?

Joel: Let's start with the most influential person that I got to meet here on earth. He's no longer with us, but that would-be Zig Ziglar. I read his stuff when I was a young adult. I read *See You at the Top* as I was entering into a direct sales career, and *Secrets of Closing the Sale*. I went to his Born to Win conference back in 1988.

If I had the capacity and room to take in something new, certainly there's some people that I admire, but I can't really put my finger on any mentors right now. A lot of people, and I won't name names, that others look up to, I've had the—I'm not sure with the privilege or just fortunate to have to gotten close with some of them. I bite my tongue because some of the people that are really respected I find unworthy of the respect they're getting. It makes me sad, because people just like to have their ears tickled a lot of times. If it makes me feel good, or it sounds good, then it must be true, and I just don't have time for posers, and I never want to be one.

I always want to be the guy that when you need me, that I'm the same guy and I don't take myself so seriously. Yes, I use the accolades that I've earned in a business way because if you had a *New York Times* bestselling book, you're like, hey, I'm a *New York Times* bestselling author, for whatever people think of that. But when you meet me, it's not like I'm somehow better or smarter because of that. No. I did the right thing, at the right time, with the right people, at the right place, that worked out great.

I'm blessed for that, but I'm a pretty fallible person. I would rather people know that because we identify with people who fail, right? We identify with people who fail with dignity and don't look at it as though, oh my gosh, I failed. No, I love to fail. That means I'm trying stuff. It means I'm alive, doing, and experimenting. If you're not failing in some stuff, then what are you doing? There's no way you're getting a home run until you get off the bed. It's just not happening. And if you're telling people you are, you are a faker. You need to take off that dumb mask and try and just be who you are, instead of trying to prove to other people that you somehow have it all together, because I know and you know and God knows that you don't.

Tony: So Joel, what's in the future? I know it's hard. I asked you this at dinner about a month ago. Looking at the next year or two, what do you see Joel Comm doing? What's the next chapter beyond video for Joel Comm?

Joel: I'm more interested in inspiring people. That to me is far more interesting and exciting and rewarding than teaching them . . . We can give anybody information. They teach people how to do this, but in order for people to remember what you're teaching them, you have to touch them emotionally. You have to touch the heart. There needs to be an inspiration for some that need the motivation, but there also needs to be an emotional connection. And I hope that that's what's happening now as we're speaking and as people listen to this, as they read this book and share the story, or watch my TEDx talk, that they will be inspired.

Because if I haven't inspired you, it doesn't matter what I've taught you. If I haven't inspired you, it doesn't matter if I've made you laugh. What matters is if what I have shared with you makes you stop and think about something in your life that you want to (d0) different or whether it tells you that the path you're on is the right path. But if listening to me doesn't inspire in your soul some sort of change, that you go, "Oh, if this guy can do this, then so can I." Right? That's it right there. That's the nut. If this guy can do this, then so can I. And you can, because I'm not so special. We are all unique. I'm gifted in certain areas, but believe me, if we go down the list of the things I can do and the things I can't do, the can't list just goes on and on and on and on. I kid you not.

Five Key "Mind Nuggets" from Joel to Ponder and Reflect Upon

1. *"We've been trained to get want we want, when we want. Well, now along comes the ability for anybody to broadcast and people can consume what they want, when they want through live video. The big players are the usual suspects: Facebook, YouTube, Twitter, but there's going to be more coming on the scene."*

2. *"While we have a preponderance of information, a well of data and knowledge, we are sorely lacking in wisdom and discernment. Knowledge if having information. Wisdom is knowing what to do with it. I just hope more people will take time to discern what it is they're doing."*

3. *"When I look now at who my mentors are, I guess I don't really look at my peers as mentors. I feel like life just teaches me. I try to be a student of whoever is sharing what they're sharing."*

4. *"I love to fail. That means I'm trying stuff. It means I'm alive and doing and experimenting. If you're not failing in some stuff, then what are you doing? There's no way you're getting a home run until you get off the bed. It's just not happening."*

5. *"We can give anybody information . . . but in order for people to remember what you're teaching them, you have to touch them emotionally. You have to touch the heart. There needs to be an inspiration for some that need motivation, but there needs to be an emotional connection."*

What Else Joel Revealed During Our Interview

Here are a few more of the areas we discussed during our *Captured Wisdom* audio interview, which can be accessed at www.mindcapturebook.com/interviews:

- *Why the perfect storm has arrived with mobile technology and the ability to create video*

- *Marketing lessons learned from the 2007 Internet show and contest* The Next Internet Millionaire
- *The power of being positive and effective ways to avoid being negative online*
- *Why you should avoid being a keyboard cowboy*
- *The lessons in authenticity from the TEDx keynote speech in Denver*
- *The power of mentors and how meeting Zig Ziglar changed his life*
- *Why asking questions and maintaining curiosity is such an important mindset to possess*

About the Social Media Trailblazer, Joel Comm

Joel Comm has been on the frontlines of live video online since 2008. Joel is the leading voice in live video marketing. Whether using tools such as Facebook Live, Periscope, Instagram, or Snapchat to broadcast a clearly defined message to a receptive audience or leveraging the power of webinar and meeting technologies such as BeLive.tv or Crowdcast.io, Joel's tested strategies make him an in-demand speaker and consultant for brands both large and small.

Joel is The New York Times bestselling author of fifteen books, including The AdSense Code, Click Here to Order: Stories from the World's Most Successful Entrepreneurs, KaChing: How to Run an Online Business that Pays and Pays, and Twitter Power 3.0. He is a contributor to Forbes, Inc., Entrepreneur, and the Social Media Examiner, and his work has appeared in The New York Times, on Jon Stewart's The Daily Show, CNN, MSNBC, Fox News, and many other places.

Joel has been building online businesses since 1995. His first website was amongst the first 18,000 sites in the world, and his efforts have brought experience in creating and selling websites, licensing content, affiliate marketing, Internet marketing, blogging, podcasting, online video creation, social media marketing, joint ventures, mobile app creation and marketing, authoring books, public speaking, conducting live training events, and more.

He also hosted and produced the world's first competitive Internet reality show, The Next Internet Millionaire.

For more information, visit:
Joelcomm.com

CHAPTER 7
DAN KENNEDY

"The entire explosion of media has fragmented the audience."
—Dan Kennedy

Marketing Trailblazer

There's not a day that goes by where I don't think of Dan Kennedy's advice and wisdom in relation to my own business and thoughts on marketing. I've been around what many clients and fans of his work call "Planet Dan" for more than twenty years now. I've devoured his books. I've attended countless seminars he's led and have successfully put multiple tips and strategies he's shared into action within my own business and with many of my direct clients.

His no BS approach to marketing and mentorship have helped me in two highly competitive industries (telecom and advertising) before venturing out on my own with my own publishing and training company. I must say that I was blessed and fortunate to meet him at a young age and bond quickly with his Midwestern style and results-oriented philosophy of direct marketing versus traditional advertising or image marketing.

His results and track record over the past forty-plus years in the direct response and copywriting arena are legendary. They call him the millionaire maker for a reason. With a wide variety of people in multiple industries seeking the opportunity to work with him time and time again, he commands big fees and in many cases a piece of earnings tied to increased sales and equity within a company to even consider choosing to work with a potential client. That's gutsy. Bold. That's Dan Kennedy.

His results are legendary. If you ask almost any veteran direct marketer both online and offline, they will not only tell you how good Dan is at his craft, but that he's also someone they've learned from and take very seriously. I'm not kidding when I say that he's an alchemist who can write magnetic-style marketing copy that not only gets *Mind Capture*, but bottom line: big results for many of his clients.

The three main things I enjoyed most about my interview with Dan include:

1. He made a brutal assessment of why a crowded media universe, especially online, is not only making it harder to get attention but to keep clients coming back again.

2. For a large part of the interview, we discussed how Amazon is dominating not just across the board, but the impact it's having on profit margins with a lot of brick-and-mortar firms. In short, very few businesses are safe anymore from the impact Amazon is having on purchasing and profit margins.

3. Dan built discipline into his daily life to not just write and create great marketing copy, but more importantly, to live the

life of autonomy and freedom he chooses on his terms versus chasing down business.

Key Highlights from Our Interview

Tony: Dan, you and I had a conversation a few years ago at your home about the Amazon effect. You know Amazon.com is massively disrupting everything in every industry, including a lot of the infomercial market. How do you compete against an Amazon? Do you join or die?

Dan: Well, if you can be Amazon, buy Amazon or someone like it. If you can be Amazon, and there is any significant money in what it is that you do, you will be Amazon'd. It is only a question of when. It is not a question of if. The possibility of it not happening has now passed. My level of certainty of that has really locked in. One thing you do is you hedge against your own destruction.

Tony: That's a great quote, by the way: "Hedge against your own destruction."

Dan: I own a lot of Amazon stock, and it has appreciated substantially since I bought it, and I bought it at the point that I became absolutely certain that there was no question about the fact that if you can be Amazon'd, you will be Amazon'd. So, you either have to be in something so micro specific weird—

Tony: Tiny niche.

Dan: Yes, that Amazon doesn't ever get to, or you'll have to be delivering something that they either never will, or it will be forever before they can replace you or sell to somebody. An example: hearing aids. Their days are numbered because they're digital. The only thing that keeps Miracle Ear, Beltone, and audiologists in existence is that you got to go back three or four times to get them adjusted perfectly until they work.

Tony: It's more the service than the maintenance.

Dan: The minute that can be jacked into an app and the adjustments can be done at a distance, those guys are all dead. It's over because right now that $8,000 sale will be a $280 sale. It'll be over just like smoke detectors used to be $800. They were sold in a home like fire alarms . . . so their days are numbered.

Another example: dentistry. It's going to be real hard to do dentistry online at a distance. Now what Amazon can do is step in front of the selection of the dentist, which they're doing. Amazon and Google now see themselves as becoming portals.

Tony: Toll booths?

Dan: Yes. Amazon and Google intend to own those businesses, insurance and so forth. Dentistry is very hard to eliminate. Pizza, they're going to pay hell to have a pizza pop out of your iPhone. You can order it on your iPhone, but . . . so you got to be in that or you got to be selling to people who are in that. So, you got to be selling to a protected species, right? You got to be able to live with it in a co-petitive rather than competitive manner.

I have a couple clients that this is the primary driver of the business right now. So, they have a full-scale Amazon store. So, if you're going to have an Amazon store, Amazon has all these internal mechanisms that govern how you get featured or not featured, whether you can have video on it or not have video on it, because Amazon is a search engine. They're Google for buyers.

They're a search engine for buyers. It's what they are. They are, so they make all these decisions about whether you get traffic or not, right? Just as Walgreens decides whether they are going to put a product on the shelf or not, based on what the manufacturer is doing that drive sales, people into Walgreens to want it.

Tony: Do you think (it) is harder now to compete as a marketer than when you played the game full time or not?

Dan: It's just different. In some respects, it's easy, and in some respects, it's harder. So, the explosion of media and with it the explosion of technology has in many respects made it easier. Certainly, for speed— if we want to run a test and we want to test six headlines and pick a winner, we can get that done in a day. In real time, we can rotate them. We can drive traffic to them. For example, what you had to do in 1980 to get a newsletter in the mail compared to what you do today to get a newsletter in the mail because of technology is easier.

In many respects, the tech has made it easier, faster, and cheaper to be a marketer. The explosion of media has removed a lot of the middle men. Talk about book publishers, right? There is still a role for real publishers. There are still reasons for authors to want to be published by real publishers, but it's not necessary. It once was essential. The only way you got there was you had to get an agent and the agent had to get you a publisher. And there's only so many slots, and that's it, right?

Now you can ebook publish yourself. You can publish on the Amazon platform. There is all this media, right? That's all made it, if you want to use the word "easier," it has all made it easier.

Now, at the same time, the same stuff has made it harder. For one thing, it has erased all barriers to entry. It's harder and harder to have what's called a moat around your business, which is the criteria for what Warren Buffett invests in. Where is the moat? It is harder and harder to put a moat around a business. The speed to knock off is much faster, right? Even a decade ago, if you got an infomercial on the air that (was) working for example, you had about ten to twelve months before anybody could catch up.

Tony: That was your head start before the knock-offs.

Dan: Knocking you off, right? It's a month, right? Online—it's faster. That brings with it its own cost and complications. The audience is incredibly fragmented.

Tony: Shiny.

Dan: Well, fragmented.

Tony: And shiny. It's my platform. How in the hell is anyone going to pay attention anymore?

Dan: That's right. The entire explosion of media has fragmented the audience.

Tony: Time for two more quick questions. Keeping it on schedule here, Dan. These are very personal questions I've been wanting to ask for a long time. We've had private conversations, not taped. At this stage, what gives you the most joy in your life?

Dan: You know it is a version of another question I was just asked. There is no good answer to it. I even think it's a lot objective. I'm not a big I-want-to-be-happy guy. I really prefer to be productive. There is nearly nothing I do that I would do if I wasn't getting paid. There is nearly nothing that I enjoy so much that I would do it for free, but my price is autonomy. So, everybody has to decide what their top prize is that they're willing to trade anything and everything in order to achieve. For somebody that might be celebratory joy. It's not for me.

Mine is autonomy. To the extent that I am achieving autonomy, I guess you can say I'm getting the most joy out of life and I'm pretty effective at it and have been pretty effective at it for a good span of time.

Tony: Awesome. Final question, thirty, forty years from now . . .

Dan: I will be dead . . . I'd like the last check to bounce as the old joke goes.

Tony: I've heard that. What would you want someone to say about Dan, or how would you like to be remembered? I know that's not an easy question.

Dan: Oh no, it's a very easy question. I don't care. I know a lot of people care deeply about this, and if that motivates them, great. It does not matter to me one wit, so I really don't care what anybody thinks about me now. What you think of me is really none of my business. I do my thing. Howard Stern took a call from a guy who wanted to give him helpful criticism. I will get you a copy. It's about eleven minutes long, and it is fabulous because Howard explains why he doesn't want it and the guy trying to wrap his head around the fact that . . .

Tony: It's not going to make a difference.

Dan: He doesn't want it. I mean it's hilarious, but it's really instructive . . . I really don't care now, so why would I care when I'm dead, right?

Tony: It is over at that point.

Dan: I resonate with some people, I repel others. I'm happy for the ones I resonate with. I am utterly undisturbed with the ones I don't resonate with. Howard Stern's answer was said differently, but largely the same.

Tony: Same context.

Dan: I mean, I do my thing, and I do it to the best of my ability because I care about that, and I do it in a way that is autonomous, that it is non-interfered with in any way, shape, or form. The rest of it kind of is irrelevant to me.

Tony: One final thing: Does it still shock you what you have achieved at times? I mean I've read the stories. I've been on Planet Dan for twenty years. The people you've met?

Dan: I think shock is the wrong word, because for the most part it's what I set out to achieve.

Tony: It was a plan.

Dan: But what impresses me, if you want to say it that way, is what so many people have achieved who give me some measure of credit as to following me in one way, shape, or form. Collectively, we literally have changed the way business owners think about business, advertising, marketing, sales, wealth, in hundreds of business categories with enough depth, to enough of a market share, that it is visible and known and influential in those industries. But, I haven't done it. I may have caused it.

Five Key "Mind Nuggets" from Dan to Ponder and Reflect Upon

1. *"Amazon is a search engine. They're Google for buyers."*
2. *"It's harder and harder to have a moat around your business. Where is the moat? It's harder and harder to put a moat around a business. The speed to knock off is much faster."*
3. *"To the extent that I am achieving autonomy, I guess you can say I'm getting the most joy out of life and I'm pretty effective at it and have been pretty effective at if for a good span of time."*
4. *"You've got to be able to live in a co-petitive rather than competitive manner."*
5. *"In many respects, the tech has made it easier, faster, and cheaper to be a marketer. The explosion of media has removed a lot of the middle men."*

What Else Dan Revealed During Our Interview

Here are a few more of the areas we discussed during our *Captured Wisdom* audio interview, which can be accessed at www.mindcapturebook.com/interviews:

- *Why Amazon is such a dominant force that all industries should take into consideration*
- *The impact speed to market is having on all businesses regardless of product or service*
- *How Amazon is not just an online place to shop, but frankly a huge search engine*
- *Time shifting and how it's impacting not just buying, but attention*
- *Why most businesses miss out on referrals*

- *Foolish beliefs about entitlement when it comes to growing a business*
- *The power of autonomy and doing things on your own terms*

About the Marketing Trailblazer, Dan Kennedy

Dan S. Kennedy is the provocative, truth-telling author of seven popular No B.S. books, thirteen business books total; a serial, successful, multimillionaire entrepreneur; trusted marketing advisor, consultant, and coach to hundreds of private entrepreneurial clients running businesses from one million dollars to one billion dollars in size; and he influences well over one million independent business owners annually through his newsletters, tele-coaching programs, local chapters and Kennedy Study Groups meeting in over 100 cities, and a network of top-niched consultants in nearly 150 business and industry categories and professions.

Dan lives in Ohio and in northern Virginia with his wife, Carla, and their Million Dollar Dog. He owns, races, and drives professionally in about 100 harness races a year at Northfield Park near Cleveland, Ohio.

For more information visit:

Gkic.com

CHAPTER 8
JEFFREY GITOMER

"The biggest frustration that I have are salespeople using sales techniques trying to find the pain, trying to overcome objections, trying to probe. The old way of selling is so far dead, it's not even funny, and when you walk into somebody's place, they already know who you are. They already know your reputation."
—Jeffrey Gitomer

Sales Trailblazer

I've been a fan of Jeffrey's work for almost twenty years. He is one of the top sales trainers in the world who not only had a prolific writing and speaking career, but has also been way ahead of the curve when it comes to social media. When he released the book *Social Boom! How to Master Business Social Media,* he was once again thinking ahead of others.

What I enjoyed most about reading his book *Social Boom!* was that he also enlisted several leading experts within social media to reveal simple and effective ways to make it work more effectively for any business or organization. This shows wisdom, as this topic is not only confusing to most people, but it is also changing constantly as new channels of communication within it seem to pop up every week.

Something else that has always impressed me over the years watching Jeffrey's career blossom is how hard this man works and that he never rests on his past successes. He has a strong inner drive, discipline, and energy to keep creating, teaching, and sharing wisdom with others at a very high level. This not only shows the sign of a true pro, but is also inspiring.

Besides the book, it's also worth noting that Gitomer has built up a very large, loyal audience of followers and book buyers over the years by providing great content on a consistent and regular basis. This also demonstrates that attracting, engaging, and connecting with people on a daily basis via the use of social media is of high importance and can no longer be ignored.

The three main things I enjoyed most about my interview with Jeffrey include:

1. He's not only direct, but he is very real. You always know where you stand with him. What you see and hear is what you can expect.
2. Jeffrey walks the talk. Our interview was about his book *Social Boom!* and how to use social media more effectively. He uses it very well and is still active in the day-to-day managing of it versus delegating it all. He still has a pulse to the ground and interacts with his clients and readers.
3. Jeffrey still has the energy and drive to make things happen. He's now sixty-eight years young and still writing, speaking,

and teaching. This is not only amazing, but it shows that he truly loves what he's doing. This is not so true for many writers who break through and attempt to coast along the rest of their careers without stepping up their game.

Key Highlights from Our Interview

Tony: You really jumped into this (social media) full time about two years ago, and what I'm curious (about), Jeffrey, is I like to ask questions that most interviewers will not, and I don't like softball pitches because I get interviewed all the time as well. What's one of the biggest challenges you have in social media? And then I want you to flip it on what's one of the biggest opportunities you see?

Jeffrey: First of all, my biggest challenge is maintaining my authenticity. I have a lot to do and I'm a very time-giving person and sometimes I don't always have time to respond to the people, but I don't want to give it to somebody else. I don't want to let someone else handle my social media. That's my biggest challenge because I want to be able to respond to my customers, and sometimes I'm on the plane for ten hours and I've a crazy travel life. So, I try my best within the framework of what I've got to maintain my authenticity.

Second of all, the biggest opportunity is that social media is instant. It's a couple years old in the mind of most people. Jump in now and start to build your awareness and your customer base or your follower base while it's still young.

Tony: Let's talk about the new standard on page twenty. I'm going to dig right back in the great book *Social Boom! How to Master Business Social Media.* On page twenty, Jeffrey, you talked about these new standards by which you'll be evaluated, granted appointment time, decided upon, measured, branded, and talked about what are they and why they are important.

Jeffrey: Well if you are a salesperson and you're going out on a sales call, if you're calling on me and you want to sell me a $100,000 . . . something—it doesn't matter what it is, health insurance or a new condo something—before you ever walk in my door, you're going to Google me. Well if you come you think, I'm not going to Google you. You think I'm not going to Facebook you, look you up in LinkedIn or Twitter, and check out your YouTube awareness. I'm going to find out exactly who you are way before you enter my presence, and you can't stop me. And the people are going to say, "Twitter, I'm not going to bother with it." Why would I want to teach them what's new when they don't even know what's old?

Tony: Huge.

Jeffrey: I don't think you have a choice.

Tony: Well if you look at page twenty, Jeffrey . . . you talked about just those two or three factors, but you had a lot more different resources in here that people might thought a word of mouth. They can freak out and determine in fifteen seconds are you relevant or are you a relic.

Jeffrey: Exactly. So, I only look at it in my standpoint people are going to find out about you or they can go on my Wikipedia page and find out all about me. You can go to my YouTube channel, you can subscribe to my email magazine. You can go to my blog, or you can go to my website. I'm relevant on the Internet in every aspect of it and so much to anyone else who wants to be there in the business world five years from now.

Tony: Jay Abraham is one of my marketing heroes. One of my favorite Jay Abraham quotes is "It's better to be loved or hated than tolerated." And I remember when he laughed when I asked him that question about why he came up with that, but if you're not doing some things out there to make riffles or capture people, you're not doing anything.

Jeffrey: The challenge that anybody has with social media is they try to go out and do what someone else has done. Stop that. Go out and document all of your own knowledge. What do you know? What does your customer know, and what does your customer want to know and start to interact with them on that basis. But for me, Tony, the most powerful things when customers post about me, they get one on one with me. And that way I can respond to them in a way that everyone wants to see. They want to see that I'm a huge being the same way I want to see the Dell or Zappos or Procter & Gamble response to their customers one on one. That's what makes social media work. It's not an ad on television that goes for three seconds and costs you $300,000 and you have no idea what it's worth. You went to some round-table discussion with the bunch of people that (said) *oh, this is really good*, and then the advertising agency puts you there. It's not worth jack anymore.

Tony: Correct.

Jeffrey: All these newspapers and all these televisions or radio stations are scrambling and struggling because their revenues had been cut or more, and the reason is social networking. Why? Why would I put an ad in a newspaper about how great I am when I can just talk to my customers and they'll tell somebody else.

Tony: Exactly. I mean, well you've done brilliantly and also a form of a kudos again as a fellow speaker and author you've gone direct. Seth Godin, when I interviewed him last summer, he did that as well with his latest book. He's bypassing traditional publishers and going direct to his customers, and he's having success with that. But he built an audience first before he cut the cord.

Jeffrey: Yeah, everyone needs to get feedback from their customers, but they need to have relevant feedback that's for all other customers to see. When you have one of those inside focus groups, ten people come around, give you their opinion, and then they put an ad (on) television, and it's absolutely stupid and worthless. And an advertising agency, in my opinion, their word is probably as successful as anybody else's is because I sat one day with the chief marketing officer from Capital One. When they presented the idea of "What's in Your Wallet" to the ad agency, the ad agency called it dumb. And let me say the *former* ad agency called it dumb.

Tony: Yeah.

Jeffrey: So that's the kind of crap you get. There's no accounting for the most brilliant minds in the world because I will guarantee you right now that the biggest advertising agency on the planet has a Twitter follower somewhere around zero or less because they decided not to get involved so they don't look embarrassed that they couldn't gain any followers because they have nothing to say.

Tony: If the rules have changed, what is your biggest frustration when you trained sales team people about cold calling?

Jeffrey: The biggest frustration that I have are salespeople using sales techniques trying to find the pain, trying to close the sale, trying to overcome objections, trying to probe. The old way of selling is so far dead, it's not even funny. When you walk into somebody's place, they already know who you are. They already know your reputation. They've already banged every computer research on you on the planet. The bottom line is you're not prepared for them anymore. You're prepared with your staff, not their stuff, and they don't care about your stuff. They only care about their stuff.

Tony: What is some of your teaching foundation, and why is this relevant to our audience?

Jeffrey: First of all, let me give you a big picture. I wake up in the morning and I write, and what I write appears in my other bricks. I blog, I have an email magazine. I write an article every week. I write books. Those are bricks that help me create attraction outside of social media. What you do outside of social media will determine your success inside of social media . . . I give public talks, and you know I appear around the country and those that help me build my network of interested people and that's the challenge.

You can't just go on Twitter and say, "Here I am," and expect a hundred people are going to show up. They're not going to show up. They're going to show up based on the fact that they already like you, and they already believe in you and they're already confident and they already trust you. Then they'll follow you. But in the book I tell you, you have to create attraction. You have to engage people well enough and speak enough to where they want to connect with you, and the secret word is "value." Attract, engage, connect with value.

What I did is I just gave you my thought process or my philosophy of social media. You attract people. You engage people, and if you're attracting well enough and you're engaging well enough, then they'll connect with you. If you attract them, and you can't engage them, they're off. If you attract them and engage them and you can't connect with them, they're off. And the secret butter or the secret sauce is value.

Tony: If someone came up to you and he said, "Jeffrey, what do you want to be remembered for as far as your speaking and publishing," (what would you say)?

Jeffrey: Well the legacy obviously is the books that I left behind that have been successful. The reason that I am successful like I am is because I write like I speak, and I'm real world. Nobody can read a book of mine and go, "Jeez, I wonder what he means by that." No, I'm brutal in the face purely in New York and that bullshit-New-York-real Manhattan, not Rochester or Albany. I'm getting pissed from the perspective of I'm going to be either ran away but I'm not going to be plugged. I'm going to tell you exactly how I feel about something so you can form your own opinion. I'm not saying I'm right all the time, but I'm saying if you have a different opinion from mine, you'll know what your different opinion is, you won't have to guess what mine is.

Five Key "Mind Nuggets" from Jeffrey to Ponder and Reflect Upon

1. *"So I'm pretty prolific in the area of social media because it works. It works for me and the most amazing age has just nothing to do with it. Stupidity has everything to do with it. The companies that are not involved or sticking one foot in the water or one toe in the water are stupid or they have lawyers that are even stupider."*

2. *"First of all, my biggest challenge is maintaining my authenticity. I have a lot to do and I'm a very time-giving person and sometimes I don't always have time to respond to the people, but I don't want to give it to somebody else. I don't want to let someone else handle my social media."*

3. *"Well if you are a salesperson and you're going out on a sales call, if you're calling on me and you want to sell me a $100,000 . . . something—it doesn't matter what it is, health insurance or a new condo something—before you ever walk in my door, you're going to Google me. Well if you come, you think I'm not going to Google you? You think I'm not going to Facebook you, look you up in LinkedIn or Twitter, and check out your YouTube awareness? I'm going to find out exactly who you are way before you enter my presence, and you can't stop me."*

4. *The challenge that anybody has with social media is they try to go out and do what someone else has done. Stop that. Go out and document all of your own knowledge. What do you know? What does your customer know and what does your customer want to know and start to interact with them on that basis."*

5. *"I'm going to tell you exactly how I feel about something so you can form your own opinion. I'm not saying I'm right all the time, but I'm saying if you have a different opinion from mine, you'll know what your different opinion is, you won't have to guess what mine is."*

What Else Jeffrey Revealed During Our Interview

Here are a few more of the areas we discussed during our *Captured Wisdom* audio interview, which can be accessed at www.mindcapturebook.com/interviews:

- *Why anyone can get involved with social media regardless of age or background*
- *The power of LinkedIn within today's competitive job market*
- *How to engage and connect with your clients and prospects using social media*
- *Why one-on-one engagement makes social media stick and relevant*
- *How social media is disrupting the old media models such as TV and radio*
- *The power of testimonials in building online social proof*
- *Effective ways to attract, engage, and connect with value*

About Sales Trailblazer, Jeffrey Gitomer

Jeffrey Gitomer is the author of The New York Times *best sellers* The Sales Bible, The Little Red Book of Selling, The Little Black Book of Connections, *and* The Little Gold Book of YES! Attitude.

All of his books have been number one best sellers on Amazon.com, including Customer Satisfaction is Worthless, Customer Loyalty is Priceless, The Little Red Book of Sales Answers, The Little Green Book of Getting Your Way, The Little Platinum Book of Cha-Ching!, The Little Teal Book of Trust, Social BOOM!, *and* The Little Book of Leadership, *and* 21.5 Unbreakable Laws of Selling. *Jeffrey's books have appeared on best-seller lists more than 850 times and have sold millions of copies worldwide.*

For more information visit:
http://jeffreygitomer.com

CHAPTER 9
JAY ABRAHAM

"They can actually grow a business in a recession of tough economy like this—10 percent, 20 percent, 30 percent, 50 percent—when everybody else is dropping 30 percent, 40 percent, 50 percent. It's very possible, but it requires a shift in paradigm. It requires a different mindset."

—Jay Abraham

Strategy Trailblazer

Jay Abraham has been called the Marketing Wizard and with good reason. When someone can sit down and in five minutes or less come up with multiple new ways to generate new and repeat business, regardless of product or service, this to me is not only a rare gift, but about as close to magic as you can get.

I was super blessed to sit down a few years ago at the height of the global recession and discuss the forthcoming book titled, *The Sticking Point Solution: 9 Ways to Move Your Business from Stagnation to Stunning Growth in Tough Economic Times.* If the title of the book didn't grab you, I can tell you that the wisdom inside the book certainly will. With Jay being one of the highest-priced marketing consultants on the planet, at $5,000 per hour, I was honored to get thirty-five minutes on the phone with him to discuss key marketing strategies for my listeners.

To say I did my homework for our interview would be a massive understatement. Being a fan of his work for over twenty years and knowing how rare it was to get an interview, I poured through my notes taken from his book and crystallized them into a short, tight list that I believed would be of relevance.

The three main things I enjoyed most about my interview with Jay include:

1. Jay has a deep understanding that marketing is the fuel that keeps all organizations running. A common thread in each person interviewed in the book is that they are extremely effective at marketing their ideas.

2. Jay has a unique perspective that business can grow exponentially if it employs a good mix of marketing initiatives and utilizes joint ventures. Joint-venture marketing is rarely employed by small business. On the other hand, large companies use it quite effectively to not only share resources but to help attract and retain more customers.

3. Jay believes in building relationships with customers for life and that staying in front of them is of huge importance. I work with a lot of clients and the number-one mistake I often see is customer neglect. Not in the literal sense, but in relation to staying in touch with them. The mission is to keep growing the

business, and the smartest way to do it is through continual communication with happy customers to keep them updated on ways we can continue to serve them along with reminding them that we appreciate their business.

Key Highlights from Our Interview

Tony: Jay, I have been a big fan of your book for many, many years. It's interesting. You charge, I believe arguably, the highest consulting fee in the marketing profession. How do you get people to gladly pay this fee, especially now? A lot of people are cutting back on their marketing. How do you do that? What is your secret-bullet plan, as you would say in Jay Abraham universe?

Jay: Thank you for that. Well, there's two actually, Tony. The first is one that you can't fake, and that's what I've really done. I've been in the front lines of capitalism for thirty years, and I've been involved in 465 industries, not businesses, and I've personally been involved in engineering, orchestrating, analyzing, refining, course-correcting over 50,000 different selling, marketing, advertising, lead generating, product service, one-step, two-step, multistep, online, offline, direct selling, indirect selling activities.

So, when I interact with a prospective business, a client, I can ask them questions about their business, about the performance, about factors in their business that they've never asked themselves. And it's very, very clearly apparent that I really understand my business—it's not going to sound real humble—but at a seminal level that most people don't. And then secondly, we look together at what the economic impact should and could be of what I would do for them before they commit so that we can clearly establish that the return on their investment would be at multiples of 100 percent or 1,000 percent, so that it's a no-brainer.

If it's a really big challenge sometimes, I'll let somebody have a little, not only give them a deal, but I'll give them terms because it's not funny. It's more of a fun game for me. I don't mean it disrespectfully. But yeah, we're here to serve. Basically, if somebody spends, let's call it $40,000 one time, but they get a $200,000 improvement that recurs every year for life in their business, and that $200,000 of extra profit can buy them $1 million or $2 million or $10 million home or another business or liquidate their debt or move them and their family to a higher sort of a life stratosphere, it's a pretty cheap one-time investment.

Tony: It's fascinating to me to look at your new book, how you crystallized, as you would say, front-line marketing down at a street level and you've got the track record to do it.

Jay: It depends on how your career plays out. I've had the good fortune of concentrating most of my work, Tony, in the small/medium entrepreneurial world. I've done some big corporations and major publications and some very iconic entrepreneurs. But the vast majority is the small/medium entrepreneurs. And they've got different opportunities, they've got more passion, but they have different challenges, one of which is they don't have the capital, nor the resources, nor the infrastructure, nor the team. They don't have the talent.

And they've got to basically sort of zig when everyone else zags. They need greater guidance, and they need to be liberated to realize they have a lot more control of their economic and their competitive destiny than they really think.

Tony: Why do you think marketing is the ultimate leverage or skill for any organization to master?

Jay: It was very interesting because I did an interview earlier today with a really, really bright guy, somebody who's very renowned in the marketing circles, and he's one of my—I admire him. And he was quoting somebody that I quote too, and it's Peter Drucker, who's deceased, and was probably the greatest management and business consultant that ever lived. And he basically said the purpose of a business is very simple: It's to acquire and sustain customers and buyers. And he said there's only two elements in business that make profit: marketing and innovation.

Marketing and innovation generate business; everything else is an expense. Marketing is the greatest leverage in the world, and I'll tell you why and you probably have already taught this, so I'm probably being redundant, Tony.

If you can get ads or you can get letters or you can get commercials or you can get emails or you can get paid advertising or organic search that was generating X to generate 3X, if you can get prospects that were converting at 5 percent to 15 percent. If you can get sales that used to be $50 to move up to $85. If you can get buyers that were buying one time to buy three times a year. If you can get the people that didn't buy in the past to be repurposed and monetize them in another honorable and ethical way, the combined impact that can have in your business is geometric.

I mean it can be thousands of percent. If you look at my track record, I'm very proud of it. I've had a number of clients or students or protégés whose businesses have exploded hundreds or thousands of percent. Everyone thinks it's smoke and mirrors. It isn't. But most people limit and restrict and impede their achievements and success because they don't demand the maximum performance capable of the marketing.

Last thing I'll say is that in the marketing arena, in the revenue-generating aspect of a business, there are normally ten to thirty different leverage or impact points, each one of which can be improved anywhere from 10 percent to 2,100 percent, 10 percent improvement to twenty-one times improvement. Well, if you can improve twenty-five revenue elements in your business by only 15 percent, the combined impact is hundreds or even a 1,000 percent. And most people don't recognize, Tony, the power of geometry to boost the profit performance of the business, even in bad times.

One of the things that I think I've been blessed to be able to do is help small-, medium-sized entrepreneurs—we're all marketers, either bad ones or non-marketing, but we're all marketing. And if you realize that you had so much more control of your destiny. You know, I was talking on an interview that I was doing with somebody else about two hours ago, and I said, "Here's the real gaping hole that most small, medium entrepreneurs don't grasp right now. Their industry can be down dramatically—30 percent, 40 percent, even 50 percent, Tony. And I think the world is over and the sky is falling. But if they can develop a strategy that, first of all, adds so much value that they don't lose their existing recurring buyer base; if they can figure out how to telegraph so much more value to the marketplace that their competitors—top people who are value-based flock to them because all the competitors are retracting and withdrawing services and value—and if they can telegraph to all the new people coming into the market that they've got the best possible solution or product service for the need, they're going to grow when everybody else is dying."

They can actually grow a business in a recession or tough economy like this—10 percent, 20 percent, 30 percent, 50 percent—when everybody else is dropping 30 percent, 40 percent, 50 percent. It's very possible, but it requires a shift in paradigm. It requires a different mindset. It requires recognizing and harnessing the powerful forces that have always been available to every entrepreneur listening and just using it to its maximum ethical advantage.

Tony: Jay, let's talk about endorsements and testimonials. On page thirty-five, you really hammered this home. Why are they so critical in the persuasion process to use endorsements and testimonials?

Jay: People who know my work, and you'd be one of them, know that I've done billions of dollars of increased revenue and profits for clients. And about half of all the achievements I've done were based on finding another business or an influential organization or a publication or an affinity group in a marketplace that already had spent years and millions or tens of millions of dollars to build the trust, the credibility, and the belief with their marketplace that they could just tell that market, "Hey, you can trust Tony," or "You can trust Jay," and that they would follow that.

And basically, for a fraction of the effort, for a fraction of the cost, for a fraction of the time, you can own a market. We do five-day training programs on power partnering and the power of endorsement. But the bottom line is leverage. It's ethical leverage, Tony. Why would you want to go in the outside market and spend an enormous amount of time on ads or calling cold on prospects trying to get them to trust you when you can instantly gain trust by getting someone) they already deal with and respect to say, "Tony, somebody who can help you is unimpeachably honorable, trustworthy, and he delivers."

When they do that, all of a sudden you own it. There's a great story, and it's told about five different ways. I've already told about Rockefeller, Baron, Rothschild, Bernard Baruch, depends on how old you are. I'm sixty, so you've got a lot of different things. But the concept is somebody wanted to borrow a large sum of money from them. Rockefeller, Bernard Baruch from the '30s, and Rothschild. And Rothschild said, "I will not lend you the money you want, but I'll do something far more valuable. I'll walk arm in arm across the stock market floor with you twice— once there, once back, and once again. And when I'm done doing that, everybody will loan you all the money you want." And that's the essence.

Tony: Yeah. Well, something that I learned from you as a pup when I was twenty years old, Jay, is risk reversal. And really, you beautifully summed up what they're doing is leveraging risk reversal and opportunity cost to educating that value and not be a vendor. But they know the payoffs are in multiples.

Jay: Yeah. And their attitude is it's only a matter of time before everybody that they want as a client will affirmatively become one. And they're not going to wait for money to change hands before they start investing to make that chiropractor's practice healthier, more prosperous, less stressful, more sustainable. And that's a great attitude. I admire them a lot. Truly I've had an influence in their philosophy, but I really admire that. There's so many interesting companies.

There's a really good book that you might tell your people to read. I think it's called *Small Giants*. And it's by a guy named Bo Burlingham. He's the editor-at-large of *Inc.* magazine. He studied all these companies that chose to remain, relatively speaking, small but be great at what they did. And I think he chronicled fifty really cool companies, as small as two-person companies and as large as 500-person, but nothing big.

And he found that those people had a better vision, a better sort of a world view of what they wanted to mean in the marketplace. It's pretty cool. That's a book I think will help people see what great small companies look like, because I suspect, and I'm not demeaning, but I suspect if you're like the people that I work with, you've got a lot of really passionate small- and medium-sized entrepreneurs listening to this and working with you.

And their challenges, their opportunities, their plate, their purpose, their situation is decisively different than that of the big corporate behemoth. Their passions are richer. Their challenges are decisively different. And I think that book would be very useful for them.

Tony: Again, ladies and gentlemen, listening in all over the world, we have the author Jay Abraham of the *Sticking Point Solution*. After you read ten copies for you and your closest associates, go out and get *Small Giants*.

Jay: I have nothing to gain, but I'm very impressed with the work of this man. He's a very passionate champion of the role of entrepreneurs in the world, and he's done some incredible, incredible research and refined reporting of things that can make entrepreneurs' lives richer and more prosperous. And I just really admire the guy. So, you might want to do that because it's great, and it's called *Small Giants*.

Tony: What do you mean by the strategy of preeminence? It's one of your sticking trademarks here. Pages thirty-nine and forty in the book really nail it. What do you mean by preeminence for our audience?

Jay: Well, it starts with a sad realization. The vast majority of businesses in the world, particularly small and medium, have been marginalized, commoditized, and rendered basically non-distinct and really almost, not useless, but just a parity type of a provider by two separate factions. The consumers want to bring them down to their knees so there's no ability to charge a premium, and their competitors want to bring them to their knees.

And if you can see that, then you're basically on a depth now, you know a spiral, until what we try to do is establish every company we ever work with a positioning of being the preeminent provider in their marketplace. And preeminence takes on many different points of view, but the first thing it always is, is that they establish themselves as the most trusted advisor in the niche or in the category or in the role they take for life for the clients that they serve.

The second is they shift—and I talked about it earlier. They don't fall in love with their product or their company or their technology. They fall in love with the people that their product or service helps. And they love to see those people's lives better off because they were in it.

Number three is they provide very well-reasoned advice. They don't just give information. Number four, they see their role as being this continuous enhancement of people's lives with every communication, whether it's a letter, an email, a visit, a call, a technical question.

Whatever it is, they try to make everyone that they deal with live better. Third is they treat people as clients, not as customers. A customer, if you look up the Webster dictionary definition, is somebody who buys a commodity or service. A client is somebody under the protection, the well-being, the—there's another word, I can't think of it. It's like a fiduciary experience. And they have a distinct understanding that there are three categories, four categories actually, of clients they serve. The first one, of course, are the people that pay them.

The other three are the people they pay—their team members, their vendors, and their advisors. And they want those people in their lives to grow, to thrive, because their goal is not just to pay the least and use somebody the most who's an employee. They want to see that employee thrive and grow and evolve and have the happiest, richest life) so that they will give back to their clients. So, they're very enlightened, and they're playing a totally different game.

And they're getting a much greater fulfillment or a much greater satisfaction. They're operating in a more rarefied stratosphere like facet of the business world than anybody else they compete against. I don't know if that is too esoteric or if that makes sense.

Tony: You can go either way on this question. You can go positive or you can give a warning. What are some of the biggest mistakes businesses are making right now that drive you crazy, or what are some of the biggest opportunities that they can take advantage of? So, you can go biggest mistake or challenge, or the biggest opportunity for businesses right now circa mid-2009.

Jay: Well the mistakes are, first of all, letting themselves be marginalized. The second is being tactical and reactive instead of strategic and proactive. The third is that they're not really reinvesting in marketing and really distinguishing what value, what benefit, what superior and incomparable advantage they can give. They're not availing themselves of all the resources they could out there and setting up relationships where people get paid more for the performance or the value, not just a fee.

They're not really trying to be innovative. And innovative is not necessarily technological. It means coming up with better ways to really impact and add value to the market. Innovative can mean better marketing. Innovative can be new and improved versions of the product. Innovative can be taking away the risk. Innovative can be supporting the client. I think that right now people feel so paralyzed, hamstrung, marginalized, and beleaguered that they're not sticking their head out of the morass and seeing that they really don't have a lot of preeminent and really preemptive competitors.

They just got a bunch of people who are groveling as they're being engulfed in the quicksand of this bad economy and are desperately trying to stay in business. But you can extract yourself and really put yourself in the catbird position if you stop really doing what everyone else is doing. And speaking of that, most people, when they get into a bad situation like this economy, they just keep doing more of what didn't work. And a good economy means some of the most—let's say it politely—some of the ludicrous and not very productive things get massed because a rising tide lifts all boats.

That's what happened in the boom times. In the bad times, like the emperor's new clothes, you're transparent, you see that your marketing doesn't work. Your selling doesn't work. Your positioning doesn't work. Your strategy or lack of it doesn't work. And the problem is most small and medium businesses get so scared they just do more of what doesn't work. They've got to break out of that chain and say, "Whoa! I need to approach it differently. I've got to be more strategic. I've got to test and see what does work. I've got to try new approaches."

There's a concept that I quote all the time. People need to be—they need to make propositions that are irresistible, and they need to be positioned to where they are unbeatable. But most businesses are beatable and resistible, and that's a big problem.

Tony: Folks, *The Sticking Point Solution* by Jay Abraham—right time, right book, right place. It's a definite piece to get you on that track. So, Jay, an honor and a privilege. You are the marketing genius, I will give you that, and I don't say that lightly. But I appreciate you putting this into a book that people can get it and really turn this economy around.

Jay: Thank you, Tony. That's very gracious, and thank you for being such a good advocate of my work. I'm very, very appreciative of that.

Tony: Host-beneficiary at its best. Jay, it's been a pleasure. A continued success to you.

Jay: Thank you.

Five Key "Mind Nuggets" from Jay to Ponder and Reflect Upon

1. *"We sat down and said okay. Let's try to come up with some universal sort of principles, elements, and levers, leverage points that would get any small, medium-sized business or professional and private practice unstuck. And we worked through it for the better of six months of really reducing and simplifying it. But we had a feeling the economy was going to falter. We didn't know it would implode. So that's what got me to do it. I wanted to help people who were stuck get unstuck."*

2. *"So when I interact with a prospective business, a client, I can ask them questions about their business, about the performance, about factors in their business that they've never asked themselves."*

3. *"So migration just refers, Tony, to the process of advancing and enhancing the transaction forward and continually making it a recurring transaction if it's such a highly repurchasable product or service, or moving them up to different support or combinations or collaborative products or services that'll make their life or their business better."*

4. *"And when you're the most trusted advisor, you have a point of view. People are silently begging to be led by somebody who has a very, very well supported point of view who they can trust, who*

they can trust because that person has the consumer's' best interest at heart."

5. *"There's a concept that I quote all the time. People need to make propositions that are irresistible, and they need to be positioned to where they are unbeatable. But most businesses are beatable and resistible, and that's a big problem."*

What Else Jay Revealed During Our Interview

Here are a few more of the areas we discussed during our *Captured Wisdom* audio interview, which can be accessed at www.mindcapturebook.com/interviews:

- *How to look at your business in a new way to help increase profits*
- *Effective ways to leverage joint ventures to build credibility and new business*
- *The four essential areas most businesses get stuck in and how to improve them*
- *The process of migration in relation to current customers to keep them coming back again and again*
- *The ten to thirty leverage points that drive revenue in most businesses and ways to improve upon them for increased revenue*
- *Why you must position yourself in the market as the trusted advisor and proven ways to do it*
- *The power of marketing in every organization and why it's so valuable*

About Strategy Trailblazer, Jay Abraham

Jay Abraham is currently the founder and CEO of Abraham Group in Los Angeles, California. He spent the last 25 years solving problems and has significantly increased the bottom line sales for over 10,000 clients in more than 400 industries worldwide. He's won high praise as a marketing genius in *USA Today, The New York Times, The Los Angeles Times, The Washington Post, San Francisco Chronicle, National Underwriter Entrepreneurs Success,* and the list goes on and on in many of the publications.

Jay's clients range from business royalty to small business owners, many of whom acknowledge that his efforts and ideas have led to an increase in profits ranging into the millions of dollars. He is also an author and his latest book is titled, *The Sticking Point Solution: 9 Ways to Move Your Business from Stagnation to Stunning Growth in Tough Economic Times.* He currently lives in Los Angeles.

For more information visit:
http://abraham.com

CHAPTER 10

SALLY HOGSHEAD

"Our attention span is getting shorter, but our customers' attention span is getting shorter, and the second your customers' attention is diverted away to anything other than you, your message and your product, now allows your competition a chance to swoop in and attract them. And so, distraction is your greatest enemy in sales."

—Sally Hogshead

Fascination Trailblazer

Sally Hogshead has been called the Queen of Fascination. When I sat down to interview her and discuss her book *Fascinate: Your 7 Triggers to Persuasion and Captivation*, little did I know that our interview would be one of the most memorable I've ever conducted. Not only is Sally wickedly smart, but she's also down to earth. I found that our interview

101

time flew by. It seemed like we were old pals who'd known each other for years.

In her book *Fascinate*, she revealed a wide variety of insights into such areas as why the Salem witch trials began with the same fixations as those in *Sex and the City*, how a 1636 frenzy over Dutch tulip bulbs perfectly mirrored the 2006 real estate bubble, and why the billion-dollar "Just Say No" program actually increased drug use among teens by activating the same "forbidden fruit" syndrome as a Victoria's Secret catalog. If these topics don't capture your imagination, not much else will.

Since we first spoke, Sally has gone on to even greater heights of success and hit *The New York Times* bestseller list in the summer of 2014 with her book *How the World Sees You*. She is not only a great marketer, but her extensive research and passion in the areas of persuasion and marketing have placed her in very rare company as one of the world's top experts on the subjects.

The three main things I enjoyed most about my interview with Sally include:

1. She did her homework on the topic and had the data to back up many of her points. In addition, her resume of working with many of the biggest brands in the world gives her a unique and valuable perspective on the mind of consumer behavior.
2. Sally talked about beverages and how something as nasty and potent as the drink Jägermeister can not only still exist but actually thrive. It's a great case study about the fact that even the strangest of products can make it with good marketing and a unique audience.
3. Sally shared the lesson about vanilla ice cream and why it's still so popular in a world and industry loaded with tons of options and competition.

Key Highlights from Our Interview

Tony: I want to start up and really dive into your book *Fascinate: Your 7 Triggers to Persuasion and Captivation*, and I know you travel around the world doing keynotes. In branding you do all sorts of really cool stuff we're going to talk about. Why is fascination so important for businesses to understand and apply?

Sally: I will need to persuade at some level. We all need to captivate somebody, and fascination is the most intense form of focus. You know what this feels like Tony, when you're having your conversation with somebody and they're completely consumed in what you're saying. They're totally focused on you. They're not thinking about their voicemails and emails. They're not thinking about Twitter and Facebook or what they're going to serve their kids for dinner. They're completely focused on what you're saying at that moment.

And that's when you have somebody, when you have that kind of connection with somebody in this moment they're not distracted, that you're not competing with all the other messages around. That's when you have the ability to actually start to persuade them. That's when you can connect with them when you can get them to fall in love with you, get them to fall in love with your message, with your product, when you have the greatest likelihood to sell them, and most importantly, it's when you have the greatest likelihood of developing a real relationship.

Tony: I have interviewed a lot of the best authors on the planet, and the media kit you sent me, I'm going to let the audience know, is the most captivating and fascinating media kit I've ever received from an author.

Sally: Wow! Thank you.

Tony: You autographed books for me, you sent me a handwritten note. I thought, *she actually practices what she preaches, and she does (it on) a level that's just fascinated me.* So, I want to bring that up. You didn't know I was going to tell you this, Sally, but it was absolutely stunning how you captured me and again, you walk the talk. So, I'm just letting everybody know that she's the real deal.

Sally: Thank you. Well, can I tell you why? Can I tell you why it's so important for me to make sure that interaction was incredibly captivating?

Tony: Absolutely, go ahead.

Sally: . . . If you'd been born a hundred years ago, Tony, your attention span would have been about twenty minutes long because you probably would have lived on the farm. You would have (had) very few things competing for your attention. It would have been in your brain's best interest to be able to focus on a single task for a long period of time like plowing.

But then a little thing like the Internet came along. And with all of the social media and voicemails and emails and messages that are coming at us all the time, our brains are rewiring and neurologists can tell you that the BBC released the report that your attention span is probably around nine seconds. Nine seconds. So, this means that roughly every nine seconds, your brain is making a decision whether or not you are going to stay focused on me to this conversation or you're going to start looking at your BlackBerry and looking at the texts that are coming in. And it's my job if I want to sell to you, if I want to persuade you, if I want to connect with you, I have to be more fascinating than whatever it is that that's distracting you, and nowhere is this more important than sales.

In sales, it is absolutely essential that you understand how you do your natural strengths—those built-in strengths in your personality and how you use them to become persuasive so that you can capture people (with) a nine-second attention span.

Tony: Sally, that is so huge, and what I like a lot in *Fascinate* is you back it up with a lot of empirical evidence. You've got studies, and it takes us into one in particular where you talk about The Kelton Study.

Early in the book you revealed two things about fascination. Could you share with our audience what they are and the implications of that study?

Sally: Sure. I want to make sure that people understand fascination is a neurologically proven experience. You know what it's like when you lose yourself in the moment from people or we call it being in the zone. It's a peak performance experience when you're fascinated, you're totally focused. And I wanted to be able to explore this from a quantitative point of view. Another is to a piece of research that was not my opinion, that was done by a global research company named Kelton Research, one of the top in the world. And I commissioned the studies to them.

What fascinates us exactly? How do we behave when we become fascinated? When somebody is fascinated by your product, how more likely are they to buy it? How much more are they willing to pay for it? How much more are they willing to believe you and trust you and respect you and be fascinated by you?

Of course, there were thousands of pieces of data that came out of this very in-depth national research. One of the things that we learned is that products that are fascinating can charge a lot more money because people have a relationship (with them) and they are so captivated by them. They're willing to pay more money. So, the implications in sales is if you can make yourself and your product fascinating through the system that, Tony, you and I will be talking about today, the Fascinate System—if you can make yourself and your product more fascinating, you can charge more money. You can charge the premium. You can have more loyal customers, you can create more social media buzz. You can have more people with long-lasting relationships with your customers, ones that your competition cannot cut into.

The other things that we learned in a big way was that people want to be fascinated. It feels good to be fascinated. It almost feels like having a crush when you're listening to a song and you're consumed by how the music feels, when you're watching a movie and it moves you and it brings us to be fascinated. So, this is a good thing. If we can fascinate our customers, we're providing value to them that strengthens the relationship.

Tony: Let's talk about this interesting information on page seventy and seventy-one, or should I say fascinating. Describe why lust is also the same as craving, and how do marketers employ it?

Sally: Yes, lust is an irrational attraction. When we feel lust on something, there's absolutely no data or analysis. I can't explain why we feel that way. For example, you might feel lust towards a new piece of technology that you're dying to have, like the new iPhone. The new iPhone comes out—I'm going to lust about it because I'm going to hold it and use the navigation. It makes no sense at all, and I'll stand in line to get it.

Maybe you lust for a certain pair of shoes or you lust for a certain fabulous new client. It's that feeling inside of us that's totally emotionally based that makes us want to be close to something. Now in our system we change the word "lust," which applies perfectly to the brand, and now we call it "passion" because passion is more about the bond that happens between people. The point is the same on both. If you want to sell a product on a basis of attraction, do not sell on facts. Don't try to sell it on facts and data. Don't give information. Information kills desire. We want to sell it on how the person is going to feel when you have it.

In the Kelton Study that we did, we found that when somebody feels there's attraction towards (a) product, that there are actual and physical symptoms and their pulse quickens. It's almost like an adrenaline burst when they hold it in their hands. They feel a sense of craving and desire. When you place this around your brand, it makes people bonded to it and it's not a rational way.

But people begin to be willing to do nonrational things. They pay more than rational people would. They try to cross town to be able to procure it. They don't want the parity version. They don't want your old version. In a way to do this, to be able to create this kind of attraction is to build stories on to your brand, to build and to use five senses. So, imagine in your experience if you're doing a sales presentation, if you want to build this type of emotional connection of passion, one thing you might do is just not think through the bullet points and the PowerPoint presentation but instead to think through how can you invite the customer into your office? Think about the experience. How can you participate with them? Are you using good eye contact and body language? Are you turning yourself towards them so that they are open to you and you're open to them, because if you're doing these things you're persuading in some ways, in a very different way than bullet points and PowerPoint presentations. It's not that the bullet points and the PowerPoint presentations do not have points, they absolutely do. That's just a different trigger.

Tony: Let's move on to something more taboo.

Sally: You know it.

Tony: It's something that nobody likes. Then tell us why they always get it and why they talk about it.

Sally: I would love too. First, Tony, let me ask you a question, Tony. Have you ever had a shot of Jägermeister, that brown liquor?

Tony: Yes. When I read the book, I laughed out loud because it's like legendary, and we all complain how bad this product is, but like, oh my gosh, Jaeger bomb!

Sally: Exactly . . . the other good thing is that most of our listeners have at least tried it once, but very few of your listeners actually like the taste. And the reason that Jägermeister is so successful, colossally successful, and one of the top brands in the world with the number-one imported liquors in to the United States . . . (is) because we have this connotation around the brand.

It's a night of (extremes). It's a night when you're going to drink Jägermeister, you know that you're dialing in. You know that you're committing to this specific type of experience that when somebody says, "Hey, guys, let's do a round of the Jaeger bombs—or even more so—let's do a shadow ice-cold Jaeger." Immediately, so many people pop their eyes open up, "Oh, one of those nights!" So, it's a bonding tradition, and so what I propose in *Fascinate* is that it's the fact that it doesn't taste good that has increased the sales. And the lesson to take away from this for your product or for your service: It's creating fascinating products and service. This is not a function of trying to please everybody.

In fact, it might actually be doing things that turn people off that they get people to talk, they get people to want to be part of it, to be part of the culture and to share. So, there's something in the way that your point of sales is distinct. For example, if you're located in a really crappy strip mall, or if you have a really terrible time for your product delivery, how can you change that negative? So, we interpret it as a positive. So, it becomes an intrinsic part of the experience of what the customers are buying because if you can do that, it appears to be a positive just like the taste of Jägermeister seems to be a positive. It pleases to be a negative instead of bringing a positive so that you can build upon that and actually use that as a competitive advantage.

Tony: Alright, I want to rewind back in time in history. You move through and talked about trends from 1636, yes the year 1636, and something called Tulip Mania. What were the lessons you discovered from Tulip Mania?

Sally: Tulip Mania was the first economic bubble that the economists saw for our history. It was the first time there was (a) bubble that people are paying so much more for an item than it was actually worth, more than the market estimated. We see these on dotcom's where people were paying crazy prices for stocks in dotcom ventures that they didn't even know really existed yet. We saw this in a real estate market. I happened to be living in California during that bubble and watched houses quadruple in price in a period of two years, which was in a way a different phenomenon.

It is actually the first time that actually happened with the tulip of all things, as far as tulip the flower, the tulip market, and there was a bubble. The prestige trigger is the trigger that we haven't really touched on. Prestige (is) about elevated respect and about assuming that something has more value than it actually might. The prestige trigger took hold and another one when the tulip became traded publicly on the open market. If a price for an average tulip being a dollar or two, let's say suddenly the price escalated to such a radical degree that the people were paying more than the price of a fine house, simply for a tulip bulb—and the house is not worth as much as the tulip bulb planted in front of the house—now that's not making any sense. Of course it's easy for us to go back and say, "How could this possibly (have) happened?" You know a tulip bulb has no intrinsic value. It's basically a commodity that it's going to fail in three to five years. You can only say it can only boom for a fine amount of time.

You know these aren't magic tulips. It's the same ones you would buy at the grocery store—it's just beautiful. But the same principle applies. The same principle is a product can elicit the prestige trigger. That product is being perceived worth more and it actually is. It's what we see with the certain designer brands than the actual commodity value as you know handbags at not only $200 but that bag can command $2,000.

Tony: Let's end with Fortune 500 companies. Why do they shy away from controversy and want to maintain the status quo?

Sally: Awesome question. I love that, and to answer that, I'd like to talk about vanilla ice cream. I keep vanilla ice cream in my refrigerator not because I love vanilla ice cream, but because it's going to go with the maximum number of things. It's going to be eaten by the maximum number of people. And it's going to be complained about by the fewest number of people. So, if I'm having a dinner party or I'm having my family around or friends over, if I want to serve ice cream, vanilla is really a safe choice and nobody is going to get pissed off about serving vanilla. But I really like vanilla. You know that vanilla, it's pretty good. I can tolerate it, but it's in the middle of the road.

On the other hand, I really love pistachio ice cream. I love it! In fact I would rather have pistachio than anything else in the world. But the problem is, if I keep pistachio in my freezer, there are a lot of people who are not going to like it. It's going to get a lot of complaints. Imagine if I serve it, the pistachio ice cream may not go over so well. So even though if I feel very strongly about pistachio, it's really a niche product. It's only for a few people. The bigger your company gets, the more difficult it becomes for your company to create pistachio products.

The bigger you get, the more you want to grow. You need to start to appeal to the maximum number of people or at least this is the tendency as the thinking goes. You need to do the training that goes with it and you need to start to appeal to a certain number of people and alienate the fewest number of people, until what happens is, even if the company starts out as a small company, as an enterprise they create pistachios like products. Very distinct, memorable experiences. Products that couldn't be made somewhere else but come across in a certain way. They have a distinction of innovation about them, so, they're very effectively fascinating. But then the products grow, and they become more boring. They want to appeal to as many people as they can in order to prove that their huge marketing budgets are paying off and expanding globally into other regions, so they become vanilla.

The problem is if you want controversy, and if you're not being disliked by somebody, you're probably not very fascinating to anybody. The only reason why big companies can be successful by selling vanilla-ice-cream-type products and services is that they're something so big, they can afford to hammer these products and services.

If you had a 200-million-dollar advertising budget, you probably can afford to be a little boring because you're going to have some publication, and you're going to be in front of people so many times in so many places. It's okay if you're a little bit boring, because you don't have to make each interaction not boring. However, if you don't have an ad budget, if you don't have the biggest marketing budget, if you don't have the biggest market saturation, then you must be the most fascinating. You need to find a way in which your product or your service or even your own personality can be the pistachio within your category.

Five Key "Mind Nuggets" from Sally to Ponder and Reflect Upon

1. *"With all of the social media and voicemails and emails and messages that are coming at us all the time, our brains are rewiring and neurologists can tell you that the BBC released the report that your attention span is probably around nine seconds. Nine seconds. So, this means that roughly every nine seconds, your brain is making a decision whether or not you are going to stay focused on me in this conversation or you're going to start looking at your BlackBerry and the texts that are coming in."*

2. *"One of the things that we learned is that products that are fascinating can charge a lot more money because people have a relationship (with them) and they are so captivated by them. They're willing to pay more money."*

3. *"The first gold hallmark of a fascinating product, brand, or person— in other words the number-one most important way that we can distinguish if something is fascinating—is that it provokes a strong and immediate emotional reaction. It doesn't try to be lukewarm. It doesn't try to blend in. It instantly evokes some sort of responsiveness."*

4. *"Some people are going to disagree with you, and that's okay. In fact, that's actually good, because if you don't have people who*

feel really strongly, if people don't disagree with you, then there's probably nobody who's passionately agreeing with you."

5. *"So entrepreneurs and small businesses, on this note, you have the power to make your product more captivating and it can all start from you, but it doesn't happen unless you can first identify what makes you naturally fascinating and what makes your product naturally fascinating."*

What Else Sally Revealed During Our Interview

Here are a few more of the areas we discussed during our *Captured Wisdom* audio interview, which can be accessed at www.mindcapturebook.com/interviews:

- *Why big brand companies market much differently than smaller-sized firms*
- *The issue of distraction and attention spans and how it impacts marketing and the results from the BBC News*
- *Why fascination is so important for businesses to understand and employ*
- *The six hallmarks of a fascinating message*
- *The Seven Fascination Triggers, what they are and how to use them in your business*
- *The most popular product nobody likes and why it is still so successful*
- *The marketing lessons learned from the year 1636 and Tulip Mania*

About Fascination Trailblazer, Sally Hogshead

In 2006 Sally began her research on the topic of fascination, including a **groundbreaking national study** *by a global market research firm. Her research uncovered that the average attention span is now only 9 seconds, and that the brain is hardwired to focus on 7 specific types of messages. Her clients have included Intel, Cisco, Million Dollar Round Table, GE,*

New York Life, YPO, Inc. Magazine Leadership, and Intuit, with audiences ranging from Fortune 500 CEOs to entrepreneurs in Saudi Arabia.

Sally has published several books and the interview is from her second book, FASCINATE, *was published around the globe, earning Sally a frequent spotlight in major media including* Today Show *and the* New York Times.

Sally's latest book, How the World Sees You, *released in 2014 and made the coveted* New York Times *bestseller list. In it, she explores the science of fascination, based on Hogshead's decade of research with hundreds of thousands of participants, including Fortune 500 teams, hundreds of small businesses, and over a thousand C-level executives.*

For more information visit:
http://sallyhogshead.com

CHAPTER 11
BRIAN TRACY

"The turning point in my life was when I realized that you can learn skills that would make you more valuable and you could dramatically increase your income. Then I went from literally sleeping on the floor of a person's one-bedroom apartment to having my own car and flying around on jets within twelve months with that discovery."

—Brian Tracy

Communication Trailblazer

It's amazing to me that sometimes when we try too hard to make things happen, the effort and time are for naught, and we initially feel like we're fighting a losing battle. On the other hand, sometimes when we seek to make something happen, it simply might take a few hours or days to occur, and often when we least expect it. When the second scenario occurs, it often feels *way too easy!* I believe that when it comes to making things happen, it often boils down to two major things: **timing** and **intentions**.

For example, when I received an email, out of the blue, from Brian Tracy's publicist regarding his new book and that he was conducting interviews, I experienced what I described above.

A little time warp: Late last year, I approached Brian's team about a possible interview for one of his other books. After filling out an extensive media questionnaire, I received back a kind and polite "no" to my request. I was baffled, to say the least. Being under deadline, I refocused my efforts on another possible guest from my list and continued on. When the email from his publicist showed up, I grinned and immediately thought, *perfect **timing**!*

When we look at my earlier request to interview Brian, I now believe that my intention was very different from Brian's, thus the original "no" to my interview request. I was looking to interview Brian, but not only was the timing not yet right, but my intention to discuss one of his older books wasn't a fit. When Brian's publicist realized he needed to promote his new book (as a fellow author, I do the same thing) our **intentions** found alignment and harmony.

I was honored to secure the legendary Brian Tracy for a special interview to discuss his latest book, *Earn What You're Really Worth*, and other success-related topics. It wasn't easy, but it was definitely worth it as you're about to discover!

The three main things I enjoyed most about my interview with Brian include:

1. Brian has a relentless drive to keep improving and learning. It would be easy for someone with his massive success to coast after a certain period of time. This is definitely not the case with him.

2. Brian has a positive belief in the free-enterprise system. It's easy to pick on the US these days, and Brian definitely is a defender of the opportunities provided to citizens who live and do business here. It's amazing how many immigrants come to the US and end up leading successful lives under the flag of freedom, which protects and rewards their hard work and hustle.

3. He described in vivid detail the steps needed to help a person achieve a goal. I consider Brian to be one of the top teachers and writers in the business space, and to hear him break the formula down was not only a cool experience, but also an honor for a serious fan of personal development like myself.

Key Highlights from Our Interview

Tony: Let's come out and talk about your brand-new book titled *Earn What You're Really Worth.* You come out swinging in the beginning of the book, Brian, and I love this. You said, "There are three major factors that are disrupting our economic lives." Brian, what are those three things you wrote in the book and why are they important to set the stage for your book?

Brian: Well, to set the stage for setting the stage, the turning point in my life was when I realized that you can learn skills that would make you more valuable and you could dramatically increase your income. Then I (went) from literally sleeping on the floor of a person's one-bedroom apartment to having my own apartment, to my own car, and flying around on jets within twelve months with that discovery. Now the three factors to answer your question, the three factors that are affecting our life are, first of all, the growth in information and knowledge. They say that knowledge in every field is doubling every two to three years—in some fields, just every two to three months. Since the book was written, I came across statistics that the total amount of knowledge enjoyed by human beings on earth will be doubling every seventy-two hours by the year 2020.

Tony: Wow, that's incredible.

Brian: Yeah, you could take all the knowledge in the world and you put it on (a) pile and next to that pile in seventy-two hours there'll be another pile the same size and then next to that pile in seventy-two hours later another pile equally both of those piles and doubled. I mean, it's beyond our imagination. When I started writing books, Tony—I've read that they're publishing a hundred thousand books a year and only 1 percent every year are really brought to market and so on—and then that's when I got in. It's going to its highest at 200,000. Last year they published two million fifty thousand books in the United States alone in English.

Tony: Wow! And, Brian, the game has changed. You talked about this information explosion, a couple other things that are major in disrupting the economy.

Brian: Well, the second is technology. Technology is transforming our economy at a faster rate than we ever thought was possible. A very simple example: They came out with the idea of the iPod, which led to the iPhone, which led to the iPad. This year, from 2010 to 2012, they will sell a hundred million iPads, and the majority of those who buy iPads are readers. And so, what they do is they go out and buy books. And once you start reading books on iPads, you don't buy books on paper anymore, and within a year Borders, one of the oldest and the biggest bookstore companies in the world, collapsed, within a year of the introduction of the iPad. What is happening? That answers one piece of thousands of disruptive technology.

And the third part is competition. Everybody in the world is competing to enjoy a great standard of living.

Tony: You talked about in the beginning of the book that many people are living in what you described as Alice in Wonderland existences when it comes to jobs, career, and economy. What do you mean by that?

Brian: Well, it means that they don't understand that their earning is their most valuable, single financial asset. And what they're doing is really costing. They have a limited education, mostly in subjects that nobody cares about. That they came and learned a little while they're in college, if they ever went to college, they're doing the very least they're always told. They do the very least possible. They come at the very last minute. They leave the first minute, they waste 50 percent of their time during the day chatting with other workers and playing on social media and then they wonder why they have no future. They're living in a fantasyland.

Well, there's the top 20 percent of people who have a different world view. People at the bottom 80 percent have basically flatlined according to twenty-five years of research at the University of Florida in Jacksonville . . . And what does this mean? It means that they just stopped improving. They do their work reasonably hard the first year of their first job to learn their skill, and then they never get any better. And they don't understand why their income doesn't go up any higher than the rate of inflation, which means they never get ahead. Seventy percent of Americans today live from paycheck to paycheck. They have no savings. A lot of people (who are) sixty years old after a lifetime of work have an average net worth of $41,000. Those days are over. The world has caught up. We are in an incredible contest that is going faster and faster, and if we do not get into this game, we will just be literally eaten alive by the competition from people more serious than we are.

Tony: You talked about early in the book a great strategy on page fifteen in relation (to) how anyone can become successful even faster. What is it?

Brian: Well, the most important thing to become successful faster is to increase your value. I put in the book a series of exercises to determine what it is that they're really good at. What have they done that (made) them successful in the past? What are the essential skills that they need to add to their skill set? And what are the things that people need to realize, I say—I used to say this, Tony—that in order for you to get to the top 10 percent of your field, you are going to work very hard for five to seven years. Very hard means you're going to have to work very hard at your work at about two hours a day, five days a week in extra-development learning, studying courses, reading, upgrading your skills. And in five to seven years, if you do that you will be in the top 10 percent of your field. You'll be one of the highest paid and most respected people in America.

And they say, "Oh my God, five to seven years. I'm thirty years old. I'll be thirty-seven years old by the time that happens." So, I always asked this question—I said, "Well let me ask you a question. How much older will you be in seven years in any case?" Seven years from now you'll be seven years older. The only question is will you be in the bottom 80 percent struggling to make a living, worried about money all the time, looking at the right-hand column of the menu to see how hungry you are when you go out for dinner when you do go out, or will you be financially independent making a fabulous living making a wonderful life? There's nothing that can stop you from getting into the top 10 percent except yourself.

Tony: You talked about why this economy and this market is tough and it's getting tougher. Why do you believe this is so, Brian, and what do you recommend people do differently to address this successfully?

Brian: Well, I wrote a book about six years ago which gets wonderful reviews which is called *Something for Nothing*. In that book, I talked about what I call the expediency factor as being basically the critically driving factor of all human behavior. Expediency factor says that people always seek the fastest and the easiest way to get the things they want right now with very little concern for secondary consequences. And it is the secondary consequences that are the most important parts of your life. So, people all want to make a lot of money and have a nice life and be happy. And today everybody is focused on what my friend Dennis Whitley calls activities that are tension relieving rather than goal achieving.

The average person is spending two to three hours a day on social media. When you're at home, you're spending three to five hours watching television. When at work, you're spending 50 percent of your time shooting the breeze, talking on the phone, playing on the computer. It's astonishing how many companies find their staff playing computer games most of the day. And what happened is the world caught up. I spend a lot of time in Asia and a lot of time in Europe. These people by the hundreds and millions and billions are extraordinarily aggressive. They want to enjoy our standards of living. They want to jump ahead of us. You know the Chinese are producing more millionaires and billionaires than any country in the world. They are so aggressive about upgrading their skills and producing valuable products and services.

The basic economic rise is you cannot consume what you don't produce. And people want to consume more than they produce. They want to actually be able to have a nice standard of living while producing little or nothing of value. And it's over. Too many people today are coasting, and the great problem, Tony, is you can only coast in one direction. You can only coast in one direction downhill. I always remember this story of this guy who jumps off a thirty-story building to commit suicide. And as he's dropping, passing the fifteenth floor, someone leans out the window and says, "How is it going?" and he says, "So far, so good." What we're doing is unreal as he's heading towards the bottom. I just had lunch with the owner of a company, and he just told me his brother is forty-five years old, college educated, (and) has been unemployed for two years. And we're talking about, how can that be? You and I and most people I know are never unemployed.

Tony: Correct.

Brian: But we're like cats. We bounce if we lose one job, we get another. We have another job on the side. We don't want to meet evenings. We're loaded with projects. We'll have so many things that we can do . . . And people say, "I've been unemployed for two years." That is a terrible statement. That means I'm a useless human being. I have no ability to render any value to anyone that I talked to. I mean, that's awful, so what do you say to people? Let's get back to education. Get back into learning.

You want to work. There's a short course called "creative job search" because that was so important and what it says, if you want to get into the industry, what you do is, you're going to interview somebody in that industry and ask what are the skills that are most in demand in this industry. And they will tell you we're looking for people that are really good in marketing, really good on the telephone, really good in customer service, and really good in sales. And what you do is you're going to learn that skill. And, Tony, one of the most wonderful things that I've learned and changed my life is that all these skills are learnable. You can learn any skill you need to learn to achieve any financial goal you could set for yourself.

Of course, everybody listening to me today could be a doctor, a lawyer, an architect, an engineer, a highly paid professional, an entrepreneur, a businessperson, a highly paid salesperson, a computer engineer, and I mean you could learn any skill.

Tony: It usually comes as a shock to some of our listeners but in chapter five, you mentioned a bold statement that, "Everybody works on commission." Why is this important for our audience to understand?

Brian: Well, this is terribly important, and sometimes I ask my audience how many people here work on commission and 10-15 percent all raise their hand, and then I'll point out that everybody does. It's because of this as a job, is it an opportunity to add a value greater than a cost of employing you? I call this a universal hiring rule. Anybody will hire someone if they feel that person will contribute more than their cost. Therefore, your job is to add value. And what you do for your paycheck or your bonus you received is merely a percentage of the value that you create. So, for every job that you do, you are getting the percentage of the value that you offer to your employer. You are working on commission.

If you want to increase your rewards, you have to increase your service. You have to serve your customer, which is your employer, with more and better and faster and cheaper things. Anybody who wants to can get a promotion. All you have to do is produce more. And you promote yourself. In fact, there's a wonderful one-liner that says, "Every time you accept a new responsibility, you promote yourself." If you want to move (up) in your career, raise your hand more. So how you do that? Start or work a little harder, stay a little later, and concentrate on the most valuable things that you can do for your employer. And your employer will willingly pay you more money. Your employer will come to you and say, "Please let me pay you more money. For heaven's sake, don't go somewhere else!"

Tony: Exactly!

Brian: What's happening today, Tony, people in the top 20 percent are increasing their income on an average of 11 percent a year.

Tony: Wow!

Brian: The bottom 80 percent are increasing their income on an average of 1 percent per year. At 11 percent per year, you double your income every 6.8 years. At 1 percent per year, you double your income, your actual buying power in seventy-two years, which is why you'll never get out and never get ahead and just stay at the bottom 20 percent.

Tony: One of my favorite books by you is *Eat That Frog* and what you bring up on pages 143 and 144. Talk about this powerful concept and why it's so effective as far as time management and product-ivity boost.

Brian: Well, some years ago, I started to study time management. I was asked to do an audio program, an audio cassette program on time management, so I said sure, I know a lot about time management. So, I sat down, and I began to pull some notes together. But I realized I didn't have six or seven hours' worth of material, so I read about thirty books on time management. I took five Time Management full-day seminars. I bought every time management system available in the United States plus Europe. And I spent a year, I drowned myself, I immersed myself in time management.

I came out on the other side with this very simple perception: It is that the quality of your life is determined by the quality of your time management, because your time is your life. And then I began diving into the keys of time management and productivity, and I found there was one key that was more important than everything else. There was a requirement that you set priorities and determine your most valuable task, but then the key is that you started immediately on your most valuable task and you stayed at it until it was done.

That's the most important key skill a person can develop if they want to live a fabulous life or (have) a lot of money to be extremely productive and move to the top of their field. It's to identify your most important task. Start on that task first thing in the morning, and then discipline yourself and stay at it until it's done.

And my friend Bob Allen says do the worst first and the worst is the biggest. It's also the one task that's more important to your future than anything else. So, what you do is you don't think about it too much. You just get up in the morning. What I do is I plan out my day in advance, and I lay out everything with my most important task in front, and when I get up in the morning I start on that. You will need that until it's done. If you can develop the habit of doing that, you'll get a fantastic burst of endorphins. When you finish the task, you feel elated and happy and you have more energy. You're moving to flow, and you think with greater clarity and you're more creative. At first people will wonder what you've been smoking, as you do your most important task first thing in the morning. It's just something wonderful. It becomes a habit. Your productivity will go up five to ten times.

Tony: Let's talk about why one's ability to focus on solutions is such a valuable skill to possess in today's economy.

Brian: It's a very good point, and I began to study this years ago. I was once asked by IBM if I would put together a program on problem-solving and decision-making, which I gave all across the country to over twenty different groups. And as I began studying the subject, I realized that success is the ability to solve problems.

Colin Powell once told me when we were speaking together on a big stage, that leadership is the ability to solve problems. In life, all that stands between you and everything that you want in the whole world are problems. A goal unachieved is a problem unsolved. An obstacle unremoved is a problem unsolved. So, the ability to solve problems is the critical skill for success in life. And if you look at people who are highly paid, every single person is a person who is very good in solving problems. You start off at a low level in an organization, and as you solve the problems, you get continually promoted as long as you solve problems. A key to answer your question is always "be focused on solutions." What are the solutions? Not who did it, who's to blame? Why did this happen? How many times? Forget all of that, and ask, "What is the solution? What do we do? What is our next step? What do we do now?" And get everybody around you thinking in terms of the solutions, and then take action. Try the solution, evaluate your results, try it again, and try something else.

All successful people are intensely solution oriented, and the more you focus on solutions, the more ideas you come up with. The more ideas you incorporate, the more endorphins your brain releases, which triggers more ideas.

Tony: Let's talk about when it's all said and done. Similar to your eulogy, what would you want people to say about your contribution to mankind? What do you want to be remembered for? Again, you've influenced millions, my friend, but if someone came to you, Brian, to write a paragraph or two, what would you really want to say or want people to remember you by?

Brian: In the simplest terms, I would want them to say in your life, Brian Tracy was a good father, a good husband, and a good friend. That's more important than anything else. If you want to expand it macrocosmically, I would say with regards to my career, Brian Tracy, he created a million millionaires for his career.

Five Key "Mind Nuggets" from Brian to Ponder and Reflect Upon

1. *"Since the book was written, I came across statistics that the total amount of knowledge enjoyed by human beings on earth will be doubling every seventy-two hours by the year 2020."*

2. *"Everybody wants four things in life, Tony. They want to earn a good living doing something that they enjoy. They want to have wonderful relationships and wonderful families with people that they love and care about who love and care about them. They want to have a wonderful health and live forever. And they want to be financially independent. Those are the big four."*

3. *"The number-one reason that people fail is they focus too much of their lives on things of low value and too little on the things that really make a difference. Restructuring is a deliberate decision to spend more and more of your time on those things that can really make a difference in your life."*

4. *"Every minute spent in planning saves ten minutes in execution. In other words, making a plan for what you're going to do before you start breaking down the steps or, in the course of your day, writing out a list of the things you're going to do that day, will save you ten*

*minutes for every minute that you spend planning. So, it gives you
a thousand percent return on investment by the very act of planning
your day in advance."*

5. *"This is a secret that will make you happy, thin, successful, and rich,
and this is: Do something every day on your most important goal.
Do something every day on your most important goal. Seven days
a week, do something every single day—and a cumulative result of
that, like a snowball gathering force, like an avalanche gathering
force—accumulative result of doing something every day starts to
give you a natural momentum, and you start to move faster and
faster towards your goal."*

What Else Brian Revealed During Our Interview

Here are a few more of the areas we discussed during our *Captured Wisdom*
audio interview, which can be accessed at www.mindcapturebook.com/
interviews:

- *Why lifelong learning is nonnegotiable*
- *The challenge of information overload and how to handle it
  effectively*
- *The proven seven-step formula for goal setting*
- *Why you should 'eat the frog' when it comes to achieving more*
- *The power of planning and other secrets to successful time
  management*
- *The three major factors that are currently disrupting the global
  economy*
- *How to make yourself more valuable in the marketplace*

About Communication Trailblazer, Brian Tracy

*Brian Tracy was born in eastern Canada in 1944 and grew up in California.
After dropping out of high school, he traveled and worked his way around*

the world, eventually visiting 80 countries on six continents. He is one of the world's premier success experts and best-selling author of more than 50 books. His extensive personal studies in business, sales, management, marketing, and economics enabled him to move up to become the head of a $265 million company before he turned his attention to consulting, training, and personal development.

He is the president of three companies with operations worldwide. Tracy is married, has four children, and lives in San Diego, California.

For more information visit:

http://briantracy.com

CHAPTER 12

BEN GAY III

"So, selling is all around you. You can ignore it at your peril or you can get good at it, and if you get good at it your personal relationships improve, from marriage on down, with your children, with your friends, with everybody, because you learn how to phrase things properly, how to make things pleasurable and easy for people to make decisions and so on."

—Ben Gay III

Influence Trailblazer

It was amazing to me, after I did research and read Ben Gay's books, to learn just how many people he's positively influenced over his forty-plus years in the selling profession. I was unaware of his work until a couple of years ago when a client referred me to him and suggested we connect. I am beyond grateful that he made this introduction.

I'll keep you in suspense, but I'll tip you off that when you read about and listen to his amazing career and influence mentioned during the beginning of our interview, you might be shocked like I was. He's hired some huge names to work with him and was personally mentored for two years by the success legend Napoleon Hill, who authored the all-time classic, *Think and Grow Rich*, which has sold in the neighborhood of over eighty-million-plus copies.

A Couple of Key Things about Ben's Books:

One, it's not every day that an author on the topic of sales comes along and frankly, floors me with his wisdom. Here's the main reason why I am so impressed by Ben's work: It's spot-on. His book series I'm referencing is called *The Closers*. Co Written by Ben Gay III in the 1970s, it's a gem, and the subsequent follow-up books in *The Closers* series, which he wrote, are just as impressive. Little did I know until I was reading his bio that the book series has sold over five-million-plus copies.

Secondly, I've been in the personal development industry a long time and have studied, read, and attended countless seminars on the topic of sales. While Ben's books were written many years ago, they are unique and contain a ton of wisdom on how to master the art of sales and effectively influencing others.

The three main things I enjoyed most about my interview with Ben include:

1. When it comes to the power of lifelong learning, Ben is one of the best examples of this principle I've ever met. His ability to stay sharp and relevant for so many years isn't a mystery. His quest for knowledge, learning, and sharing in the area of sales and marketing continues to this day.

2. Ben is friendly, warm, and approachable. With his amazing resume and the people he's met, frankly I thought he might

be a bit cocky or full of himself. Within the first sixty seconds of the interview, I felt like we were lifelong friends. Ben has a magnetic ability to charm and make people feel comfortable. This is an amazing skill and gift to possess.

3. Ben has a passion for the selling profession. He's trained hundreds of thousands of people around the globe the last forty-plus years via his books and seminars on the importance of solid, professional sales training. He's one of the true pioneers and good guys within the industry.

Key Highlights from Our Interview

Tony: So, Ben, I want to dig right in and give our global audience some perspective of what you do these days and your career as far as publishing and speaking. What's been on the Ben radar?

Ben: Well on my business card, Tony, it still says what I'm proudest of, the first talent, which was the skill that shows I'm a salesman. That's what I am at my core and always have been since age fourteen when I started my first business. In addition to that, I've added sales trainer, speaker, consultant, author, and I've written, I think, somebody told me the other day, twenty-four books. Twelve under my name, twelve for other people I've ghostwritten. So that's pretty much what I do. I speak and write and then talk to nice people like you on the phone.

As far as seminars, I'm down to twenty-four a year. I've decided I don't want to grow old on an airplane, as Zig and I were busy doing in our early days, doing 300 dates a year. I just do twenty-four a year. I don't give any speeches within fifty miles of home. I don't take any local clients. So, if I'm not on stage being Mr. Gay, I'm in Placerville, California, being Gigi's husband.

Tony: Alright, you've just mentioned somebody by the name of Zig Ziglar. Now, folks, if you haven't heard of Zig, I don't know where you've been in sales. But you fascinated me with your stories about Zig.

Tell us how you got to know each other, how you knew Zig, and your relationship with Zig Ziglar.

Ben: Well, until the day he died, within days of his death I used to kid him and always, when he was within earshot say, "That's Zig Ziglar, you know. He used to work for me." Well, I'm considerably younger than he was. I was a kid among all those people you've mentioned and several others. But I met Zig, September 15, 1965, at noon. It was a Wednesday at 1447 West Peachtree Street in Atlanta, Georgia, suite number 301. We both answered the same ad. He said if you want to make more, if you know anything about making plans, want to make more money, give me a call. I called, and Zig obviously had called. We wound up sitting in the lobby, and this gentleman named Bill Dempsey interviewed us to join an MLM company that was called Holiday Magic. Quickly it became one of the largest MLMs in the world by far. And so, Zig and I joined together as distributors.

Now he was, I think, sixteen years older than I am, as best I recall, and had already been recently successful selling cookware in South Carolina, but he wasn't Saint Zig. Nobody had heard of him unless you lived within fifty miles of him and maybe attended his church. So that was really the starting point for both of us. And then I got to be in a sales contest. The first prize was the mystery prize, second prize was a Rolls Royce, then a Lincoln Continental, and then a Thunderbird, as best as I recall. I won the contest, and Zig came in second. It turns out, I think, Zig won because he got the Rolls Royce and I became president of the company. It had its good days and bad days, and I don't think Zig ever had a bad day in the Rolls, though. So, he used to kid me and all and say, "You know you beat me in that contest, but I got the best prize."

Tony: You told me this on our first phone call about Napoleon Hill. How did you meet Dr. Hill, and what was it like to work with him directly? I mean, you've been right at the forefront witnessing history. What was Napoleon Hill like?

Ben: I was in my office when I was president of this big operation, and there stood the chairman of the board and the owner, William Penn Patrick. Next to him stood an obviously older man in not great physical condition . . . And he said, "Ben I'm bringing you a gift," and I said "Well, thank you." And so, I'm looking behind him, and it was the man standing next to him. He said, "This is Dr. Napoleon Hill," and I almost fainted because when I joined Holiday Magic at that fateful meeting, Bill Dempsey gave me two things as takeaways: One was an old, beat-up copy of *Think and Grow Rich* and the other one was a record of Earl Nightingale's *The Strangest Secret*.

Those two things he handed me changed my life to a large degree, and both men wound up working for me. So anyway, Bill said, "This is Dr. Napoleon Hill. He's going to be working for you and only for you." And of course, we went through the pleasantries, and I sat back and he said, "Call me Nappy." Then I said, "Over the next two or three years, the word 'Nappy' will never come out of my mouth while I'm standing in front of you Dr. Hill." So, we kidded about that all the time.

But he said he's going to work for you exclusively. He's going to work in complete confidence. He's not going to tell me anything you tell him or anything he tells you. You need a mentor. You're going to pass me now, and you need somebody who can teach you extra things. You need somebody else who can teach you extra things without you having to think about the ramifications. He said that Dr. Napoleon Hill is now your Catholic priest. So, he didn't have an office in our building. He stayed in South Carolina, but I saw him on a regular basis as I flew out there. He came back a few times, and we talked on the phone a couple or three times a week for that period of time.

Tony: So, Ben, let's talk about your career in network marketing and what you did. What was it like in your early days? Now, network marketing is booming, but you guys at Holiday Magic were on the front lines getting attacked probably by the FTC and the government.

How did you persist amongst all that misinformation and regulation, I would say?

Ben: Well, we had a legal department the size of most people's sales departments, held up by a lady named Dorothy Van Veralding, who was elected supervisor in San Francisco and went on to be a judge, a superior court judge. So, she was a powerhouse. And she had three attorneys working for her and lots of legal aides and so on because we got to know up close and personal every attorney general in the United States over time. The FCC, the FTC, you name it, all the alphabet agencies. And so, those of you in network marketing today, I can tell you that that process honed the industry and took off some of the rough edges, because it was sort of a Wild West.

But also, we'd fought for you to the point that you are now in business. That wasn't their goal in the beginning. The goal of the government, governments with an S on the end, was to put it out of business. It was like some sort of monster concept. Small people working from their homes and making a lot of money and so on, so there must be something wrong with it that bureaucrat heads couldn't get wrapped around it.

So, we did a lot of fighting and unfortunately, you know people would say, *Well then, where's Holiday Magic?* Though Patrick was a great guy, tremendous inspirational figure—probably the best speaker I've ever known personally, and was just a wonderful all-around guy—but he had a very stubborn streak. And when the government told him to make a couple of modifications in our marketing plan, he wouldn't make them. And I won't tell you exactly what he said since this is being recorded. But the gist of it was no.

And so at the end, I left the company because by then I'd had a falling out on how to do business. And after he taught me how to do business, we had a falling out because he didn't agree with that anymore, and he needed more money for his various hobbies and so on . . . And so anyway, he wouldn't compromise with them, and the end result was the company lingered on another year, year and a half after his death, almost three years after I left, and it finally crashed and burned.

But again, the path we forged and the battles we fought and won—some that we lost—made possible the industry that stands today. Well, Amway, for instance, at our peak was probably half our size. At some point, figures came to me. I forgot what was in the conversation with Richard at Amway or Dr. Shaklee whoever, but there was a time when we were bigger than Amway and Shaklee combined. Not as they are today, but as they were then. But the difference was Shaklee and Amway bowed to certain requests the governments made, and they survived and Holiday Magic didn't.

Tony: What do top salespeople do differently that we can all learn from, Ben? You've trained the best in the world and have been side by side with them. What do they do differently even in the twenty-first century that amazes you?

Ben: They learn the basics. In this day, as you know, MLM marketing when I first got in, we went out and talked to people face to face. Now everybody brags about sitting around in their bathrobes on their computers, which is lovely because the numbers work for you. If you can contact hundreds of thousands of people with a click of a button, something is bound to happen. But, when they get in a situation they have to learn how to sell, or have to sell, or close a sale, they can't do it. It's like the people who send all their correspondence via tweets and Twitter, and so on, they can't spell, they can't write. The social skills fade and so on. So now we have a generation of people, many exceptions within them, but a generation of people who never learned how to sell.

So, step one is they don't know the basics, so they're not going to ever be master closers or sales infiltrators at the highest level of selling. So, with that established, the best salespeople in the world follow a couple of secrets. They solve 85 percent of all the problems in selling by this simple trick: They sell quality products and services that are competitively priced to qualified people. They spend their day in front of qualified people.

To give you a quick example, if I was going to go into car selling, I would not sell Yugos, even though they're not around anymore but I hear they're coming back. The disaster that Yugoslavia tried to thrust on us a few years ago with the cheapest cars in America—it was cheap because it was the cheapest car ever built in the history of mankind. I used to laugh they had rear-window defrosters so your hands wouldn't get cold when you're pushing them.

So, if I'm going to go into automobile sales, I'd go sell Cadillacs or Rolls Royce or Lincolns or, you know, whatever BMWs—quality products that are competitively priced. And I spend my time talking to people who can afford them. I don't jump in a pool with the Yugos of the industry or whatever industry we're talking about.

I do a lot of work in the timeshare business. They greet you, give you a tour, and within two and half hours encourage you to turn over about $24,000 of your hard-earned money. The most successful people in that business are the friendliest, the most likable people you would ever meet. I've met them all over the English-speaking world, but sometimes-not-English-speaking world, who are translators.

But invariably, if I spent thirty minutes at their timeshare, I could look around and watch the others conduct their sales, and I could tell you who the top producers on the floor were. And I'm always right because they're the people you would think intuitively, instinctively you want to spend time with. So, you have to break through that. There's a chapter in *The Closers-Part 2* book which starts on page 257, called Sales Infiltration. And I lay out there in thirty or so pages exactly what a master closer sales infiltrator really does after he or she learns the fundamentals of selling.

Tony: It brings me logically to my next question. This is a big hang-up that I know you see in your audiences like I do around the world. I argue that we are all in sales. And I know that in chamber of commerce audiences where there's ministers, there's lawyers, CPAs in the audience, and they're really standoffish. Give me why you think, in your opinion, we are all in sales these days.

Ben: Well, everyone is. I work with 2,500 dentists through an association that I'm on the faculty with. And the first time I met with them I was told, "Now don't say sales to them. Say 'build the practice.' These people are not, you know, in sales. It's beneath their dignity." Now I see that may explain why many of them aren't making as much money as they should.

Let me give you an example in the dentistry business and how we now use the word "selling" openly. They even now come up to me, and they say the word (sales). We made that breakthrough at least among that little group of 2,500 of them . . . We emphasized that we're not just teaching your doctor to have an alternate choice of close, or an assumptive close, or professional close, or what have you.

It starts with the person who answers your phone. The person they approach when they get there at the front desk. The dental hygienist. The chairside assistant. You, yourself, and the lady who sets up the financing as they leave. If they're going to have enough work done with finances, they and everybody else must be part of the sales machine.

Bear Bryant—years ago at Alabama and Texas and wherever he was before even Alabama—he used to say that his job in spring training was to take fifty or sixty young men and by the end of training get them to operate with a single heartbeat. And he did many times and did very well as a result of that. But he understood it's not just the star quarterback. It's everybody on the team including the bench warmer who maybe doesn't get in until the last day of the final game and puts him in a National Championship.

Everybody has to be ready to play. So not only are we all in selling, we ought to be and we might have sales and marketing somewhere in our title. We should simply know what we're selling. Everybody is in selling . . . And as Wheelers said, "Nothing happens until somebody sells something." So, selling is all around you. You can ignore it at your peril, or you can get good at it and if you get good at it, your personal relationships improve, from marriage on down, with your children, with your friends, with everybody, because you learn how to phrase things properly, how to make things pleasurable and easy for people to make decisions and so on.

Tony: When people say to you, Ben, what would you like to be remembered for—when the final light goes out and Ben goes to the great sales party in the sky, what would you like people to remember you or your career for?

Ben: Truthfully, I'll be on the more personal note: Ben is a good husband and a good father to his three sons. On the personal level, that's the only thing that counts. But for the rest of the world, he was a good man. He did his best and loved people.

Five Key "Mind Nuggets" from Ben to Ponder and Reflect Upon

1. *"It's like the people who send all their correspondence via tweet and Twitter and so on, they can't spell, they can't write. The social skills fade and so on. So now we have a generation . . . a generation of people who never learned how to sell."*

2. *"But, you know, as it says when the teacher, or when the student, is ready, the teacher will appear. Well, if you speak in front of enough groups, there are enough people in those groups who are ready. So, it doesn't take much to ignite them. And occasionally I've been lucky enough to throw the right match into the pile, and off they went."*

3. *"I don't know if he (Zig Ziglar) had $5,000. I didn't have enough money to get my car out of the parking lot. But it's amazing what*

you can do when you're sufficiently inspired. I went and raised $5,000 in a few days, and this is 1965 dollars."

4. *"I was running the National Communications Center, and we opened the first call-nationwide-toll-free call centers in the world. So, one of those aggravating call center calls, thanks to me, they exist."*

5. *"The best salespeople in the world follow a couple of secrets. One, they solve 85 percent of all the problems in selling by this simple trick: They sell quality products and services that are competitively priced to qualified people. They spend their day in front of qualified people."*

What Else Ben Revealed During Our Interview

Here are a few more of the areas we discussed during our *Captured Wisdom* audio interview, which can be accessed at www.mindcapturebook.com/interviews:

- *What it was really like to work with, employ, and be mentored by many of the biggest personal development legends such as Napoleon Hill and Earl Nightingale*
- *His groundbreaking work within the direct-selling industry in the 1970s to take on the FTC that paved the way for it to not only survive but thrive*
- *The fascinating story behind the book series The Closers and how it sold over five million copies*
- *How he helped pioneer the call-center industry via the 800 number, which was virtually unknown in the 1970s*
- *What top salespeople do different to achieve greater success*
- *The importance of the sales process and why it's important for all employees to understand and embrace it*

About Influence Trailblazer, Ben Gay III

Ben Gay III has been called a living legend in the sales world. After 40+ years in professional selling, he has been the #1 salesperson in every organization in which he has worked. At age 27 he was president of what was then the world's largest direct sales/network marketing company, Holiday Magic. He was personally trained by fellow sales legends J. Douglas Edwards, Dr. Napoleon Hill, Earl Nightingale, William Penn Patrick, Zig Ziglar and many other sales giants.

Now one of the most famous, popular and powerful sales trainers in the world, Ben now writes/publishes/produces "The Closers" series of books, a series that is considered to be "The Foundation of Professional Selling" which has sold over 5 million copies.

Ben was the founder and is the current Executive Director of The National Association of Professional Salespeople! Ben and his lovely wife Gigi live near Lake Tahoe in the little Northern California town of Placerville, California.

For more information visit:
http://bfg3.com

CHAPTER 13
BRAD SZOLLOSE

"We were expanding so fast during the Dotcom boom that sometimes I'd see brand-new employees in the hallway every couple of weeks, and they'd look at me 'like who are you?' "Ummm, 'I'm one of the owners.' It was the craziest time I ever had in my life, and it actually seems like a dream some days because we expanded so quickly."

—Brad Szollose

Generational Trailblazer

When I read Brad Szollose's book manuscript a few years ago, I was stunned. I quickly discovered that his knowledge, wisdom, and insights picked up throughout his own life journey are not only worth noting, but, more importantly, reading and using to improve your own life, career, or business.

In his book *Liquid Leadership,* his brutal honesty is inspiring in an age of finger pointing and victim mentality that courses through many declining industries that refuse to change and grow. Yes, the old, established companies need to wake up to the fact that the radical change in how we communicate and social media are disrupting everything.

Within the excerpts from our time together and in the full audio interview, you'll quickly realize that what Brad has dubbed "liquid leadership" is why smart firms and organizations are able to compete and thrive with a diverse and changing workforce. They place a high value on people's ideas, workstyles, and influences from the different generations represented within their firms. In addition, they know that ongoing communication, training, and having a better understanding of their people's key strengths and differences helps to build an even stronger company for the future.

Brad's book and the interview serve as a powerful wakeup call and reminder that we should treat every person we work with, serve, and do business with as a valued human being capable of great ideas regardless of age or how they were raised. This is especially important for the latest group of workers, millennials, as they've been hitting the workforce full time the last few years with great ideas and a strong grasp of the new technologies.

I have some great news for you. Brad is not another boring business author who wastes your time with stories that are no longer relevant. His wit and ability to engage via powerful stories is evident during our interview and will likely capture your mind like it did mine. His insights are powerful and directly applicable from someone who's led a successful firm that was one of the first web-based firms to successfully go public on NASDAQ during the go-go 1990s while enjoying a 425 percent growth rate over a five-year period. Not many people have this on their resume, as it takes incredible hustle, persistence, and a unique skill set, which Brad shares up close and personal.

Brad speaks from the experience of hiring and managing a very diverse workforce in the city that never sleeps, New York. The bright and diverse workforce he and his partners assembled not only changed the way in which work is defined and conducted, but along the way it also gave him several insights as to how employment in the future will look. Most importantly, it revealed how leadership must address the diverse multigenerational challenges and opportunities to help build a successful company in the Digital Age.

Many of today's so-called leaders are now scratching their heads and wondering why the old leadership playbook isn't working. Brad quickly points out why it's as plain as day to see they're ignoring the elephant in the room: a diverse, multigenerational workforce.

The three main things I enjoyed most about my interview with Brad include:

1. Brad talked about drawing upon his experience of running one of the first dotcom companies to go public on NASDAQ and what he learned about hiring, managing, and working with different types of people and workstyles.
2. He has an uncanny ability to connect business, historical, and societal trends, and explain the how and why as to their
3. You can tell that he has had to hustle, adapt, and keep learning on his way up the ladder of success, as nothing was given to him on a silver platter.

Key Highlights from Our Interview

Tony: And you look at your tenure and you guys had hypergrowth and were expanding at 425 percent for five years, and so that shows me you guys weren't just a flash in the pan like most of the dotcoms—you guys had staying power. Also during that time, you had a very unique management model that really brought the first Gen Y workers to really produce documented results. In addition, your results-only work environment was so effective, motivating millennials, that you won the Arthur Andersen Enterprise Award for Best Practices. Let me repeat that, the Arthur Andersen New York Enterprise Award for Best Practices in fostering innovation among employees.

What is a generational expert? And really what do you do?

Brad: That's a good question and I wish I knew as well (chuckles). Let me back up for a second. We were expanding so fast during the Dotcom boom that sometimes I'd see brand-new employees in the hallway every couple of weeks, and they'd look at me like "Who are you?" "Ummm, I'm one of the owners." It was the craziest time I ever had in my life, and it actually seems like a dream some days because we expanded so quickly.

But let me jump in quickly as to what is a generational expert and what do I actually do. A generational expert, Tony, actually looks for the shifts and behaviors from one generation to the next and how that is affecting your business today. I'll give you a good example from the financial sector.

I had to give this keynote speech and some coaching to this financial group here on Long Island. Now you have to picture there is a room filled with these financial guys who have been in this sector for probably about thirty years, all in suits, real uptight, and the owner of the company is sitting in the front row.

Now I like to do something when I give a presentation that sort of makes them laugh but pushes the envelope a little bit. So, I chose to not wear a tie. I wore a nice suit with a handkerchief and everything, and I was real sharp, but I was giving this presentation and Sal, the owner, who is in the front row and he's turning red and ten, fifteen, twenty minutes into my speech, he's bright red. I go, "Sal, what's the problem? You look like you're going to explode." He goes, "You didn't wear a tie."

Now this bugged him to no end. I said, "Sal, I did that on purpose." He just looked at me and said, "You did that on purpose?" I go, "Yeah, I said if you go into a meeting and try to pitch the next generation and you're all dressed up just like my father did and my grandfather did, you're going to lose business because in the financial sector, especially this generation, doesn't respect mahogany walls and marble floors. Remember, they've been raised on the E-Trade, baby. They can do it themselves, and they also don't save." Now I specialize in coming in and showing companies like this how to either manage this next generation or reach that target audience that's a little younger and very different in what they value in a company.

The other thing I see mostly is that there are two problems: Either a company doesn't know they have a generational issue, or they don't know there is someone who can help them solve it and that's what I do.

Tony: So, to me, you have the boomers, and give us the age groups if you could, Brad, by boomer, Gen X, Gen Y, and millennials—give us the age breakdown, if you could.

Brad: Sure, and I want everyone to understand I'm not one of these generational experts that gives you all the details like "the traditionalists did this and the boomers did this." I'm going to give it and keep it simple for you.

Tony: Perfect.

Brad: Nineteen seventy-seven . . . Do you remember 1977? *Star Wars*, baby! Anything before 1977 is analog linear thinking and that means anyone who was born or served in World War II and anyone born after World War II are called baby boomers. Now these are marketing terms, and I don't want anyone to think that these are boxes people fit into. They're just clues to help you discern and understand behavior.

So, you have the World War II generation—the greatest generation, they're called. Then you have the baby boomers, and this goes a really long distance and that is from 1946 until 1965, in and around there.

Now the true baby boomer was raised on Vietnam and the Korean conflict. I'm a cusp baby boomer, and I was raised on Tang, the ABC Afterschool Special, and KC and the Sunshine Band, but I somehow got lumped in with this generation born after World War II. My mother was a baby boomer, and she raised me.

Now you have after 1965 to 1976, you have Generation X, which is caught right in between, and then you have 1977, which is the beginning of Generation Y. Why is this so important? Well, 1977 is actually the year that changed everything as far as raising these kids as digital kids.

Tony: Interesting. Now I'm a Gen X, so what would you say for someone in my age group that 1965 and you said up to 1976 . . . what is the tendency we might have quickly and then we can talk about the millennials.

Brad: You're responsible, but you're cynical. You don't give yourself over 100 percent to a company because you've been raised around boomers who were betrayed by Corporate America. You're part of the grunge movement beginning with Pearl Jam and bands like that. You save for retirement, but at the same time you're the generation that knows enough about the technology to be dangerous.

Tony: That's a pretty good assessment. Now let's shift into those born in '77 to the next gen, which is Gen Y, and give us some characteristics about them, and really Generation Y and millennials, why are they so different, Brad?

Brad: Generation Y is actually from 1977 to 1993, and this is roughly, but more important, millennials are the people who came of age, between eighteen and twenty-one, right around the year 2000. Those are the people who were born around 1984.

Why is that important? They don't think in linear terms. For a baby boomer like myself and a World War II vet, everything you tackle has a beginning, a middle, and an ending. Remember that, if you start a project there is a beginning, a middle, and then there's a moment when you finish that project. So, you feel good when the task is done, let's say.

But this next generation, they've been raised on hundreds if not thousands of upgrades, constant upgrades, and . . . guess what? There is no end to anything. If you've ever worked with a true Gen Y, they rush to get their work done and don't care if they make a ton of mistakes because they'll go back and fix it later; whereas) the boomer may work slower because they don't want to make any mistakes, and they do the work right the first time.

Tony: Excellent. All right, Gen Y, this is a big, big miss. You talk about generational misunderstanding, but they're motivated very differently, and it's not by money. Explain as we dive into millennials next, but what is up with that generation? Why do you think they're not into money like the old boomers think they should be?

Brad: They've been raised differently. It's a completely different mindset. Remember, they watched their parent's kind of be, for lack of a better word, they've been betrayed by corporations. They saved for retirement and bought the house, and they lost that retirement, and now they're going back to work and this generation doesn't want to have anything to do with that.

They think most of the world's problems were caused by baby boomers. So, they want to wait and figure it out by themselves, and their life/work balance is completely different. But let me delve into this. There were three big influences that changed this whole generation. Nineteen seventy-seven isn't just a date. It's a major moment in history, and I think a lot of people need to know what changed and caused this next generation to behave so differently. I'm going to dig into it, so are you ready?

Tony: This is cool because I know one of these, but the other two I'm curious to hear.

Brad: Get a pen and paper as Tony said before, because I think it's very important that everybody understand what I'm about to talk about because these three major influences will allow you to be able to know why you're doing what you're doing to motivate millennials, and it will also help you understand why you're doing what you're doing to reach customers. Let's dig in.

The first major influence was in 1977. What was the number-one box office film? You said it . . .

Tony: It was *Star Wars*.

Brad: What happened is *Star Wars* changed the mental pictures in everybody's heads of what the future was going to look like. For the first time, a science fiction movie was showing you products that were being used, and they were beat up and rough and they just fit right into that universe so comfortably.

Some of you are going to go *what are you talking about?* Well guess what? Most of the things that were in *Star Wars*—digital pads, holograms, the robots and everything—maybe we don't have a Millennium Falcon, but we do have all the other devices and they're working on the light sabers.

Tony: Yeah.

Brad: Now if you're a real baby boomer, you're going to say, "No, that didn't have the influence. It was *Star Trek*." And if you fought in World War II, you'd say it was Buck Rogers. You would both be right if you lived in an industrialized nation. But here was the big shift: *Star Wars* was the first big science fiction blockbuster to be seen all over the world. If you were in Guam or in Canada, you saw *Star Wars*. If you were in Australia or a tiny little island in the South Pacific, you saw *Star Wars*. If you lived in Russia or Japan, you saw *Star Wars*.

What it did was it put this ubiquitous image in the back of our minds that technology was cool and not something to be afraid of and it can make life better. And with this new generation then came *Star Trek*, and the rest is history.

You may not believe me, but ever since 1977, (of) the top ten blockbuster films over the last thirty-five years, seven have been science-fiction driven. So that's the first major influence . . . science fiction in the minds of anyone born after 1977 is actually science fact. It's possible.

Tony: What are the second and third influences?

Brad: The second big influence (in) 1977, and once again Atari and Magnavox brought video games into the home—now before that, a baby boomer had to go to the arcade and put quarters into the slot to pay for a video game. And along came a real silent influence that nobody was really paying attention to, and actually there were two.

I don't know if you ever did this, but there were some people where they were playing statistical baseball games using paper and pencil, and they were playing around with baseball stats, and there were Dungeons & Dragons geeks who were playing out these board games in these multilevel, multiplayer kind of ideologies.

Well these started to influence those video games, these sort of multilevel, cooler than anything, graphic-driven video cards in the machines video games, and they were entering the home and were changing the entertainment medium for a new generation.

You're probably thinking, *Come on, Brad, what's the big deal?* And in 1977, Pong was probably about the worst thing you could ever have. You're right. But it was in 1984 when Nintendo got into the game and brought us multilevel, multiplayer video games and just blew the doors off everything. Remember when Sony PlayStation and Nintendo came into the house and it was far more robust?

What do you learn when you play video games or how do you learn? That's more important.

Tony: That's a good point. It's all visual, and there are a lot of decisions, split-second and going on at the same time, and keeping track of multiple things like multiple spinning plates.

Brad: I'm going to throw out something that will blow your mind and the listeners' minds. We went from looking to the high school quarterback as the hero in our world, and we (have) now started to look at the guy who got the highest score on some video game or built a computer program as the hero.

We shifted from muscles to mind power from that moment on. Let me get back to how you learn in a video game. The first thing you learn is you have to dive in and make mistakes. You don't read a book or manual on how to play the game. You get in and make mistakes thousands of times, and that's how you learn to play the game.

How were boomers taught? Boomers were taught that if you made a mistake, your career was over. The only way to get ahead was to study hard, listen to your teachers, and your teacher would approve you and then you could move forward to the next grade. We then took that out into the real world, and we applied it to our careers. We would study hard, go to college, work our way up the ladder, and if your boss happened to notice you, you were on the fast track to moving up the ladder.

And when you got to be about forty or fifty years of age, you earned the corner office, got the big salary, you got a title, and young people would come up to you and ask you all kinds of questions because you were so awesome and you just had all this knowledge. And that is no longer working anymore! Because with the next generation, the only way to learn is you have to make mistakes. You intuitively look for your mentors and the politics and the rules intuitively as you play the game.

And then when you get to a certain level, you have to hurry up and do this as fast as possible. You kill the trolls, you storm the castle, you save the princess, and once you've done that, forget everything you just learned because at the next level the rules change.

Now does any of this behavior sound familiar? The next generation has been raised on video games, and it's the biggest influence on their brains that you can ever imagine.

Tony: Now, Brad, as the parent of three children, how does that change that? Really, I'm giving a clue for the third point, but elaborate more on that.

Brad: The one thing you're going to see, especially if you have kids, is (that) our brains, boomer brains especially, work in a linear fashion almost like a funnel. We take in as much information as we can handle. We discern what's useful and what's not useful, and we discard it. We're linear thinkers. We're funnel thinkers.

The next generation, the ones really born after 1977, their brains are actually like an amusement park. They have five ideas running at the same time with five subcategories and five other tangents they can go off on. What happens when you're at an amusement park? It's like, *Oh my God, there's a water ride! There is a rollercoaster! I want some cotton candy, or oh I have to go to the bathroom.* What happens at ten at night when the amusement park shuts down? Nobody wants to go home.

And this is the next generation. We have funnel thinkers versus amusement-park thinkers. I know the technology has been a huge influence on this next generation, but that alone along with *Star Wars* wouldn't have been the only thing that shifted behavior. It needed one more component, and that's the third component, which is child centric parenting and child centric teaching.

I have to tell you that my father was a strict Hungarian, very first generation born in the United States, and when he heard of child centric parenting, he gave it his stamp of approval. And my father had a master's degree in chemistry and a PHD, a doctorate, in chiropractic medicine, and he gave it his stamp of approval by saying it's a load of crap. That was the end of that discussion in my household.

But a lot of families, a lot of parents from that moment on, they raised their children as if they were their friends, and the hierarchy began to flatten in the household. I do this on stage—I go up to especially a female member of the audience who is old enough to know, and I go, "The conversation shifted like this, the kid started to be brought into the conversations that only adults were privy to in the past. And mothers and fathers were looking at their kid and going, 'Hey, Billy, should Mommy and Daddy get a divorce?,' 'Should we buy a new car?,' 'Should we get a second mortgage on the house?'"

I mean it sounds funny and crazy today, but that was the big shift that took place. Everybody became friends with their kids. Now not everyone did. Some people were still strict, but your kids are still going to go out into the world and meet other kids who were raised this way, and that's going to be a greater influence on them than you can possibly imagine.

Tony: Brad, let me back you up, and, as we're recording right now, I have a sixteen-year-old, a fourteen-year-old, and an eleven-year-old. I get more reaction and communication on Instagram and Facebook than I actually do sometimes physically when I'm talking to them on the phone or in person. It's funny to watch, but I get more of a snapshot of their world when I follow them on Instagram to see where they're at. There are pictures on Instagram of their friends and who they hang around with and what they're watching.

Really this is bizarre, but it's how they're raised and my kids are practically . . . what would you describe them as at that age? They're not Gen Y, Gen X, or millennial.

Brad: This is the next gen. This is a generation that doesn't even know that there's a CPU in your hard drive. They're going to save stuff in the cloud. They don't even memorize phone numbers; it's a waste of time to memorize phone numbers for this generation. They communicate easily with pictograms as easily as they can say in a text "LOL" or "See you later."

Tony: Any final thoughts for our audience?

Brad: All I can say is, "The future isn't what it used to be" as Yogi Berra said. Everything is changing, and get ready to embrace that change. I think one of the greatest quotes from *Future Shock* that Alvin Toffler ever said was this, "The illiterate of the 21st century will not be those who cannot read or write, but those who cannot learn, unlearn and relearn."

Five Key "Mind Nuggets" from Brad to Ponder and Reflect Upon

1. *"The other thing I see mostly is that there are two problems: Either a company doesn't know they have a generational issue, or they don't know there is someone who can help them solve it and that's what I do."*

2. *"Look, generational misunderstanding causes lower production, lost sales, lowers retention, and destroys your chance of a legacy. Are you ready to pass your company off to the next generation of leaders? Probably not, because you haven't trained them and they don't think like you."*

3. *"I'm going to throw out something that will blow your mind and the listeners' minds. We went from looking to the high school quarterback as the hero in our world, and we (have) now started to look at the guy who got the highest score on some video game or built a computer program as the hero."*

4. *"Studies have found that people (millennials) are not into getting the big paycheck. I mean they're not stupid, and, of course, they'll take a raise, but people want to be appreciated. That was the number-one word that stood out on every single poll they had amongst workers: appreciation."*

5. *"I really recommend that you need a safe, creative truth-telling environment. This is important. I had a friend who worked at Siemens, the largest enterprise software company in the world. He basically sat in his office down the hall from the CEO and didn't see the CEO for three years. You can't do this. People look up to the leaders. They look up to you and want to see you, but at the same time you don't want to be authoritarian."*

What Else Brad Revealed During Our Interview

Here are a few more of the areas we discussed during our *Captured Wisdom* audio interview, which can be accessed at www.mindcapturebook.com/interviews:

- *How large firms such as Dell computers are dealing with the diverse, multigenerational workforce*
- *The fascinating insights as to why TV mogul Ted Turner took classic movies and colorized them from the original black-and-white versions*
- *The massive impact that video games are having on the next wave of workers and how they view risk and failure with their jobs and career*
- *Lessons from selling in the early days of the Internet when few people really understood it*
- *The how and why of why we shifted from muscle power to mind power in the late 1970s*
- *How the shift in public education and self-esteem have greatly changed the next generation's viewpoints on employment*
- *Why appreciation has become the new carrot, not money, for motivating the next generation of workers*

About Generational Trailblazer, Brad Szollose

Brad Szollose is the author of Liquid Leadership: From Woodstock to Wikipedia. *The book explores new leadership styles and the challenges of managing today's multigenerational workforce. Brad has been an entrepreneur for more than thirty-five years and has founded eight companies in that time.*

In the '90s, before anyone knew what the Internet was, he cofounded K2 Design, the very first Internet agency, and grew it into a recognized brand with sixty employees, offices worldwide, and a valuation of twenty-six million dollars. The company was the very first Internet Agency to go public on NASDAQ. During his tenure at K2, the company grew at 425 percent for five straight years. During that time, he developed a unique management model for the first wave of Generation Y workers that was recognized by Arthur Andersen as a NY Enterprise Award Winner for Best Practices in Fostering Innovation among employees.

For more information visit:
http://bradszollose.com

ABOUT THE AUTHOR

Photo Credit Paul Jendrasiak

Tony Rubleski is the bestselling creator of the *Mind Capture* book series. He is also an in-demand keynote speaker, strategic business coach, and global event promoter. His work has been featured in various media outlets ranging from Toastmasters Magazine, The Detroit Free Press, the FOX TV network, ABC, to CNN Radio, NPR and Entrepreneur Magazine Radio. He's a 1994 graduate of Western Michigan University with a degree in marketing and has also been a faculty member and instructor with both the U.S Chamber of Commerce (IOM) and CEO Space International. His core expertise and message is designed to help people 'Capture' more minds and profits.

As editor and creator of *A Captured Mind* newsletter he has interviewed some of the highest paid direct marketing, Internet, success and sales minds in the world including Seth Godin, Jay Abraham, Dr.

Ivan Misner, Darren Hardy, Jack Canfield, Perry Marshall, Brian Tracy, Dan Kennedy, Jeffrey Gitomer, Joel Comm, Sally Hogshead, Sharon Lechter and Larry Winget.

A highly sought-after speaker and agent of change, his live seminars and keynote talks continue to receive rave reviews from meeting planners coast to coast. He's shared the stage with such business notables as Les Brown, Dan Kennedy, Michael Gerber, Jeffrey Gitomer, and Bob Burg to Olympic gold medalist Dan Jansen, and various celebrities including TV's John Walsh, Mick Fleetwood, and many others. He's presented to hundreds of audiences including some of the biggest chambers of commerce in North America, association events in the U.S. and at private events with a price tag of $2500.00+ per attendee.

Current Keynote & Seminar Topic Areas of Interest Geared Specifically to Business, Non-Profit Groups and Associations:

- *Leadership Lessons to Help You Capture More Minds and Customers*
- *Exceptional MIND CAPTURE Customer Service*
- *Referral Magic: How to Keep Your Customers Coming Back Again & Again*

FOR MORE INFORMATION:

E: tony@mindcapturegroup.com
W: www.MindCaptureGroup.com

FREE RESOURCES

OVER $300.00
In Valuable <u>FREE</u> Mind Capture Bonuses
Await you from Author Tony Rubleski:

1. The full audio interviews with Tony and ALL of the Trailblazers featured in this book along with several other bonus interviews ($300.00 value):

    To access all of the valuable audio interviews conducted by #1 bestselling author Tony Rubleski visit:

    http://www.mindcapturebook.com/interviews

2. Free report titled, 350 of the Best Headlines ever written ($20 value):

    Send an email to tony@mindcapturegroup.com with the subject line titled: 350 Report/Book Offer and we'll email you this valuable report that every marketing and sales professional should own and use to create strong marketing messages.

3. Free weekly eletter, Blog, and Facebook Updates:

    Get 'Captured' weekly with fresh updates, strategies and marketing resources designed to help you grow.

Visit us at www.MindCaptureGroup.com and click on the eletter subscriber box, Blog Tab, or follow Tony at www.Facebook.com/mindcapture.

Morgan James
Speakers Group

www.TheMorganJamesSpeakersGroup.com

We connect Morgan James published authors with live and online events and audiences who will benefit from their expertise.

Morgan James makes all of our titles available
through the Library for All Charity Organization.

www.LibraryForAll.org